Health & Healing
Through Yoga

Health & Healing Through Yoga

Anandmurti Gurumaa

Published by Gurumaa Vani

Registered Office:
57, Ajanta Apartments
36, I.P.Extension, Patparganj
Delhi - 110 092, India
info@gurumaa.com

First Published in India by Gurumaa Vani, 2010
Second Revised Edition, 2011
Photographs by Rafique Sayed

ISBN 978-93-81464-03-8

ABOUT THE AUTHOR

Anandmurti Gurumaa

Her Holiness Anandmurti Gurumaa is a contemporary, enlightened Master working relentlessly for the spiritual upliftment of mankind. Although Gurumaa herself does not bear any allegiance to any one particular religion, she is beyond that but nevertheless expounds so fluently on all major religions. Her erudite commentaries on Hindu, Buddhist, Sikh and Sufi scriptures are immensely beautiful, profound yet lucid and easy to understand. She has devised numerous techniques to aid meditation, written several books of immense wisdom and given remarkably in depth eloquent discourses on saints from different backgrounds; from Kabir, Guru Nanak, Meerabai, Sahajobai to Rumi...and the list goes on! Gautama Buddha had said, "The greatest gift is to give people your enlightenment, to dispel their ignorance." And indeed, Anandmurti Gurumaa has been unceasingly, tirelessly endeavouring to share this light of wisdom with one and all.

An embodiment of sheer love and compassion, she has been assiduously striving to teach people the art of living in bliss, in peace, breaking all the shackles of bondage, misery and suffering.

There are many facets to her truly well-rounded personality. Her mesmerising persona, a bedazzling smile enthrals and captivates one's attention completely. A brilliant musician, her mellifluous singing and chanting is totally enrapturing. A sparkling sense of humour and wit complements her razor sharp intellect perfectly. It is amazing to see people of all ages and background, men, women and children, relate to her so readily.

Furthermore, given her contemporary, modern outlook, she is especially endearing to the youth.

The main aspect of her teaching is aimed at spiritual upliftment of the masses, guiding the seeker to take steps from the darkness of ignorance to the illumination of enlightenment and freedom from all bondages and miseries of life. Moreover, amazingly Anandmurti Gurumaa is one of the rare enlightened Masters, who is able to adeptly guide all true seekers no matter which spiritual path they want to pursue (margas like gyana yoga, bhakti yoga, karma yoga or raja yoga).

Anandmurti Gurumaa puts emphasis on the art of healthy living and this book is aimed at imparting invaluable information on achieving a state of complete physical and mental well-being, a state of complete harmony. She reiterates that just because one is not sick does not mean that one is healthy! And a state of complete health can be achieved only by addressing the body and mind as one unit. An old adage says, "From the bitterness of disease man learns the sweetness of health". There is no wisdom in waiting to fall ill in order to understand the importance of good health. Hence, one ought to take adequate preventive measures.

And in this book, Anandmurti Gurumaa expounds all these measures in great depth. She says, 'Human body is a temple within which Godliness (God is neither He nor She!) resides'. Thus one has to learn means and ways to keep this body healthy and energetic. A healthy body is crucial in becoming a tool for spiritual evolution and attainment of higher wisdom. Yoga asanas, pranayama and appropriate nutritious diet are quintessential in achieving total health. An important aspect of this book is the elaborate description of the cleansing techniques which are powerful means of energising the body which in turn aids immensely in enhancing the effects of the spiritual practices.

She is based at her ashram in Gannaur (Sonepat, Haryana). There are various camps held at the ashram wherein retreats and workshops are conducted on meditation and yoga. In addition, Gurumaa does a lot of globe trotting holding discourses and meditation camps all over India and the world. The discourses, meditation camps and workshops are open to every earnest seeker irrespective of their religious or socio-economic background. It is with great compassion that she looks after all the disciples dwelling in the ashram and all seekers in general. It is indeed apt, that given the combination of her infinite higher wisdom and compassion, that she is befittingly referred to as 'Guru-Maa'!

MISSION SHAKTI

Another important cause spearheaded by Anandmurti Gurumaa is Mission Shakti - dedicated to empowering underprivileged girls so that they can lead a wholesome, dignified life with financial independence and actuate their inherent potential. This organization is non-sectarian, non-profit making and non-discriminatory. The stimulus for forming this came from Gurumaa's compassion towards the pathetic plight of girl children, especially in north India where female foeticide is rampant and prevalent age old customs and patriarchal society leads to suppression and exploitation of females on an alarmingly large scale. The core belief of Shakti is that education is pivotal in accomplishing the mission of female empowerment and changing the prevalent misguided mindset of Indian society towards the girl child and women in general. Focusing on education and vocational training is the key, as this will also address the underlying issues of illiteracy and poverty. Moreover, an educated and financially independent girl will not only support and look after her family but this will eventually lead to a better and balanced society.
For more details, logon to **www.gurumaa.com**

Twitter
Follow the master on Twitter:
www.twitter.com/gurumaa

Facebook
Visit Gurumaa Ashram on Facebook to stay updated about the programs, travels, workshops, events and discussions:
www.facebook.com/G.Ashram

G Sandesh
To get messages from the master on your mobile, subscribe to G Sandesh.
To subscribe, simply SMS
GCONNECT SUBSCRIBE <your name> to 56070

PREFACE

It is said that health is wealth. I will say that health is certainly more than wealth. Only a healthy person can actuate all innate potential and live life to its fullest, enjoy meaningfully the very essence of this wonderful gift of life.

Health is not mere absence of malady and neither does health refer only to the body. It is a state of complete equanimity and harmony of the body and mind as one unit. The loss of this 'ease' of being leads to 'dis-ease'. Health is the essential foundation on which all happiness and sense of overall well-being depends.

This book is the result of requests made by many seekers looking for an integrated tutelage covering all aspects of health and well-being, a book that is comprehensive yet simple to understand and follow. Apart from elucidating some of the common afflictions of modern times, their background, prevention and remedies to tackle their treatment, I have specifically elaborated on the various yoga asanas, pranayama and the immeasurable benefits of yoga nidra. In addition, I have expounded on the body cleansing techniques that aid immensely in not only energising the body but enhance the effects of spiritual practices.

Every human being is the writer of the script of his own life. The pursuit of being rich and wealthy or healthy and wise…? Make a prudent choice.

Love your health, love your life.

Anandmurti Gurumaa

CONTENTS

CHAPTER 1

Human Life
A Precious Gift

Human life is a precious gift and a unique blessing bestowed upon us by nature. The human body is unparalleled in the entire creation; there is no other life form which is inhabited by a similar consciousness, heart, mind and intellect. Whilst peacock, lion or cheetah are so beautiful yet they are oblivious of their own beauty. On the contrary, the peculiarity of human intellect is that even if the person is not physically beautiful, he can still understand with his intellect that 'I am beautiful and I feel beautiful'.

Infinite Possibilities of Evolution

Other living beings have the body which is controlled by nature, but the human being is endowed with the body which has intelligence, the greatest of all gifts. If we compare the parts of the human body – head, limbs, face, etc. with that of animals, we may find that these parts of their body are more attractive and beautiful than that of human body. But if we compare the human intellect with that of any other creature, decidedly the human is far superior, evolved and incomparable. There are infinite possibilities of evolution in humans, which are not possible in other living beings. From the time of their birth, to their development, until their death, animals remain animals.

The newborn baby of a human being is weak, dependant and helpless. It takes him nine months to sit up, two years to stand straight, and longer to start speaking, whereas the offspring of a cow or deer stands on its feet on the second, third, fourth or seventh day after birth, in fact by the tenth day it starts running. In other words, the physical parameters appear to develop faster and instantaneously in animals than humans, but the basic capability to receive education, the abilities of learning and thinking that are present in human beings are lacking in other living beings. The intellect of other living beings may develop over a period of time, but the intellectual advancement that is possible in humans is totally lacking in other creatures.

A tiger is born a tiger and dies a tiger. A man is born as a man but can die as a saint. The human body is indeed a marvel of superior engineering; our brain is such that no man-made computer can ever hope to compete with it and decode its intricacies. Man is the only creature who has the intelligence to aspire to and touch heights of divinity by expanding his consciousness. He can realise the divinity in himself. He can realise the creator who has created him and this entire universe. Such a realisation is not possible for any other being as the human mind and intellect are unique and not endowed to any other living being.

Now the question arises: Does man understand and recognise his uniqueness? Does he realise that his being is without parallel? Is he properly utilising his body? Or is he destroying his life by an undisciplined lifestyle? Animals die more often because of injury than of any disease - the stronger animals kill and devour the weaker ones. Yet it is true that the possibility of an animal dying of an ailment is very less. I am not referring to those animals that are city bred or domesticated. Animals living in jungles, playing in natural surroundings, are usually killed or die of wounds and injuries inflicted by other animals and not because of disease. We can conclude that animals die a natural death because being killed or eaten by a bigger animal is the order of nature - it is neither unusual nor unnatural. But it is strange that humans are dying less because of natural death and more because of self inflicted diseases.

Why Live Long?

Some yogis believe that the human body can live for five hundred years, but you must not have seen or even heard of anyone who has lived for five hundred years – it seems impossible. Around the age of forty-five man starts feeling old, and after fifty-five he feels he already has one foot in the grave. Even though compared to earlier times, these days lifespan of man has increased - he now lives longer. Medical facilities and availability of drugs have improved, leading to a greater life expectancy. But if we say that the average lifespan has increased, it would be disputable.

It is said that man's average age in this era is an astounding 120 years. What does this tell us about ourselves when the average age of a human today is merely around 50 years?

Some people feel that the average life expectancy has increased; it used to be 45 – 50 yrs and now stands at 70 yrs. But compared to the age of 500 that it used to be, it is difficult to say how significant the current increase is. If achieving the age of 500 yrs is a quantum leap, let us reduce this figure to 250, and further to 200, and still further to 150 yrs. Now how long would you like to live?

There is a very beautiful vedic shloka which says that the rishi wakes up in brahmamuhurta, and after bathing, holding water in his hands, he awaits the sun god to rise so that he can pay salutations - thus a rishi benefits from the first rays of the rising sun. With a pure mind, when he worships the sun, offering it water, he prays, "May I live for a hundred years from today." This prayer is repeated every day no matter how old he gets – 40, 60, 70, 90 or even 100 years! Thus, he is creating a determined resolve and strengthening it every day.

This determination is neither due to the attachment with the physical body or mental ties with the family, nor is it the result of servitude to home and office. This prayer of a rishi, this determination to seek a long life is in order to pursue the spiritual journey of ascending to the pinnacle of consciousness. It is a long and arduous journey. Now, with a healthy body, the presence of righteous parents, and guidance of a realised master, one has begun this spiritual journey, but it needs time to pursue until the goal is achieved. If a person dies young or falls ill, he will not be able to progress on this path, and the most important fact is that the search for 'truth' takes time - it cannot be accomplished in a day. The pursuit of 'truth' is more than a day's job!

The Search Needs Time

You attend a spiritual discourse and learn that there is something called samadhi. But can samadhi be attained in a day? You listen to the wisdom and learn about the atman and paramatma. But are these definitions enough for you? The search needs time, the austerity needs time, and so does any spiritual practice. Time is required to know and understand your own mind, your own body. Therefore, this saying of Baba Sheikh Farid is very appropriate:

Half life squandered in devouring the transient worldly things
And half in sleep
The almighty will ask
What higher purpose did you achieve?

You have squandered half your life in earning money and the other half enjoying your earnings. But the creator will one day ask you, what was the purpose of your life on earth? Was it just to build a house made of brick and mortar? To amass wealth of material goods and money? To collect metals like gold and silver that you consider precious? Do you understand the purpose of your existence? Are you even aware of it? Do you have any knowledge of the subject? The rishi prays everyday, "O Surya Dev! May I live for a hundred years from today." Why does he do this? What for? He does this because sun is the source of light and energy. This earth exists because of the existence of the sun. It is the existence of the sun that sustains our body, gives life to all vegetation, grains, fruits and flowers; plant and animal life depends on the sun; day and night, life and death are dependent on the sun. What if the sun is not there? There won't be anything!

Human life, human existence is entirely dependent on the sun. Your body functions due to the sun and your mind works due to the moon. The waxing and waning of the moon affects the human mind. After the full moon night, the moon starts waning. Philosophers and thinkers have observed that as the moon wanes, depression, sadness, worries, madness and confusion increases in human mind. It has been observed the world over, that as the full moon begins to come closer, the restlessness of psychiatric patients increases. The moon causes high and low tides and even tidal waves in the sea. On a full moon night, the tidal range is the largest. If the moon can cause tidal waves in the sea, which can further cause storm, beware as your body too is composed of 70% water. If the rays of the moon have such a deep impact on the sea, won't they have any affect on your body?

Rising at Brahmamuhurta

The moon is said to be the deity of the mind, and the sun of the body. To keep the body disease-free, the prayer for good health is addressed to the sun because the sun is closely associated with the human body. Therefore, the rishis suggested that one should pay salutations to the sun – the ruler of the body - even before it rises. Just think about this: If you are running a business or working somewhere and your superior officer is coming to visit your office, will you be absent on that day? Let me put it another way. If you have invited your revered master to your house, is it at all possible that you will not be present to welcome him? Just as the employee prepares for his boss's visit, in the same manner, we should be prepared well in advance to felicitate the sun who is the master of our body – we should rise well before sun rises in the sky.

Waking up at the time of brahmamuhurta is the best way to keep the body healthy and disease-free. The sun's rays are most beneficial especially ten minutes before sunrise; hence, those who rise early get the benefit of the first rays of the sun which are also rich in Vitamin A. When you bathe in the health-bestowing rays of the sun and absorb its energy, you become resplendent like sun. And just as the sun is a beam of magnificence and vitality, you too start becoming the reservoir of vigour and radiance. When the scholars from the west first learnt about the prayer of our rishis, "May I live for a hundred years from today", they wondered if the rishis were scared human beings. Did they fear death? Or did they desire to live long? But the rishis neither feared death nor desired to live long, nor did they have any other worries or concerns. Their only aim was to seek the unknown existence of Brahman. To this end, two situations are essential – one is to have a healthy body and second is a reasonable span of life, because nothing can be done without life and if the body is unhealthy, then too nothing can be achieved.

CHAPTER 2

Stress, Hypertension & Heart Disease

The Ill Effects of Tension

It is true that today's man has several means to make life comfortable, but along with these comforts, he has also acquired another thing - tension! Tension shakes the very foundation of your life, and the amazing fact is that the tensed person does not realise that he is tense! Ask someone if he is tense and he will reply, "No, I have no tension." But the truth is that all, from young children to teenagers and elderly people suffer from tension. Tension gives rise to high blood pressure and heart attacks. 'It seems the blood pressure is high' – this statement does not sound too alarming, but once you say 'hypertension' you realise the dangers of tension.

These days, people use the short form of hypertension - that is 'tension'. We need to have an in-depth understanding about hypertension and rising and falling of blood pressure. Understand it this way: there is a large network of blood vessels spread throughout the body; from the feet and the legs, through the spine, these vessels reach the brain while some reach the brain directly. There is a continuous blood flow in these vessels from head to toe and back again. What causes the blood to flow? Just as you have a booster in your house to pump up water, similarly, nature has fitted our body with a pump - it is the heart. There is an intricate network of ribs inside our body which securely protects the heart - it is called the ribcage. The heart is a precious organ; therefore, nature has protected it by enclosing it in a cage of bones. The heart works just like a pump.

Blood Pressure

What is the heart? It is a type of muscle which contracts and relaxes. The contraction and relaxation of these muscles causes the blood to flow in the body. The human heart not only pumps the blood in the body but also performs another important function - it channels the impure blood to the lungs where carbon dioxide is removed and oxygenated blood is returned to the heart for distribution in the body. This channelling happens through the two major blood vessels, in the upper and lower part of the heart, through which the blood enters and leaves the heart. The heart pumps this flow of blood throughout the body. The blood pressure needs to be maintained as both high and low pressures are harmful. When blood pressure is measured, both the upper and lower levels are checked.

Usually people think that the cause of headache is blood pressure, but this is not always true as the ailment of blood pressure can be asymptomatic. It is possible that your blood pressure is 200/140 yet you remain completely unaware of it - this is a very dangerous situation. High blood pressure causes symptoms but there is no certainty that the symptoms will definitely arise every time. It can produce dizziness in the head, nausea and the dangerously harmful effects of chronic blood pressure can lead to kidney failure.

Heart Attack, Heart Failure & Cerebral Stroke

High blood pressure directly affects the heart. The heart has its capacity – there is a limit to how much blood it can receive and send out at one time. High blood pressure can lead to angina (heart attack) or other heart diseases like left ventricular hypertrophy. There is an increased risk of heart failure and cerebral stroke. When the pressure of blood in the vessels is high, it is a problem, as the body is capable of handling only a certain level of pressure, that is the normal blood pressure. Suppose you install a new and more powerful booster in your house and forget that it will pump more water at a faster rate than the older one. You switch on the booster and place a mug under the tap. When you open the tap, the flow of water will sweep away the mug. This is exactly the effect suffered by the heart and brain, when the blood pressure is high. This can lead to kidney damage and even loss of eyesight. There are very fine vessels in the body that supply blood to every organ, tissue and cell. These delicate blood vessels are unable to withstand high pressures, hence, are prone to rupture leading to haemorrhage. What's brain haemorrhage? The rupture of a brain blood vessel is called brain haemorrhage and high blood pressure is a very common cause.

Let me reiterate that it is not necessary for high blood pressure to be accompanied by any symptoms like headache, dizziness, nausea or nervousness. It is a silent killer that quietly destroys your body leading you to the edge of the grave while you remain oblivious of its presence. You remain concerned with mundane routine matters like children's exam results, politics, the loan that you have given to someone and he has not returned it yet, and even cricket matches! Someone else plays the match, someone else enjoys the sport and gets the money - what do you get? Tension! You identify so strongly with all sorts of people, events, things and actions that it leads to excitement resulting in hypertension.

Effect of Unwarranted Stress on Brain

I suggest that first of all you ask yourself, whether or not, you have harboured tension within. Be honest and answer this question truthfully. Don't lie! The habit of deluding yourself is very dangerous, and it is your greatest enemy. Even accepting this seems offensive to you because you are more concerned about what others think about you. If something is not going on well at home, or there is tension in relationships, you first try to suppress it somehow so that others don't learn of it and it doesn't spread in society. Due to this desire to hide unpleasant realities, you give yourself unnecessary stress. You may desire a car, scooter, office or house, or you may have filled a tender or applied for a plot of land, or a change of job, or you may be waiting for a government license – this futile thought process about whether or not

I will be able to get desired things is not going to change the ground reality – everything happens as and when it has to happen! But by this vain thinking your brain undergoes unwarranted stress of working overtime. You may say: so what? The brain is thinking and that is its job. How does it matter? Well, it matters a lot!

Is your heart precious for you or not? Yes! Do you know that your brain governs your heart? Human brain has a vital part called the hypothalamus, which is the master computer of your body. The hypothalamus controls various functions like heart rate, blood pressure, hunger, sleep, and perspiration, and also passes the information about sensations received from the sense organs.

For example, I have this small towel in my hand - your eyes see this towel, but it is the brain which identifies it as a towel. In other words, the eyes perceive a colour and this information gets transmitted by the network of optic nerves to the brain where it is decoded and identified. So, one part of the brain understands the information received through the eyes, and another part of the brain understands the information received through the ears. Similarly, there are areas in the brain that deal with external and internal temperature, tactile sensations, olfactory sensations, taste sensations, deciphering sounds, words and body movements – there are millions of such task-specific parts of the human brain.

Importance of the Brain

Today, although modern science has an in-depth understanding of the human body, it lacks the comprehensive knowledge about the human brain. A great deal has been understood, but a lot more remains to be understood. For example, if we were to calculate the number of inputs and sensations received by the five sense organs and the five action organs in one second, we would come to the astounding figure of five billion! Even more startling is that out of these five billion pieces of information, the human brain can process only two thousand – and if we subtract two thousand from five billion, there is tremendous information that the brain does not even understand. Don't forget that these five billion impulses reach you in just one second. There are various sources through which you receive information – it is received through the skin, or may be the sound through the ears, or the view seen through the eyes...Well, right now what are you seeing?

Let me give you this assignment: while sitting here, make a mental note – later on you can write it down on a piece of paper – of how many sensations, how many pleasant and unpleasant smells, what all colours, sounds that you are receiving through your eyes, ears, nose. When you will begin to write, you will realise that it takes a long time, because your brain is bombarded with information. A host of information is coming in and the body is acting as a receiver. The network of nerves spread through the entire body is finer than a silken thread. Five billion impulses! Whereas the brain knows only two thousand! Stop thinking you are very clever, for you do not comprehend even one fourth of the five billion! Remember, we are not yet talking about infinite divinity or God, we are talking only of this visible finite world – and the brain has only limited understanding of this very world. Now all the information that is reaching the brain is processed and carried out by the hypothalamus.

The number of heartbeats per minute, the pulse rate, the blood circulation - all these are controlled by the hypothalamus. You may be learning about the term 'hypothalamus' for the first time here, completely unaware of which part of the brain this boss is located in! When you worry or you are tense, the hypothalamus, which is already under the stress of processing so much information, is further stressed by your thoughts. It is the first to be affected by your thought process, and therefore the instructions it gives to the body get affected, thus the whole system of the body goes topsy-turvy.

Be Calm and Controlled in Emergencies

Let me give you a situation - you are sitting peacefully when someone rushes in to inform you that your office has been raided - you suffer immediate stress. Or you learn of the death of a dear one – this has a direct effect on the brain, throwing the entire system out of balance and adversely affecting the body; the pulse rate will quicken, the blood pressure will rise, the heart will palpitate and the whole body will start perspiring.

Imagine being in such a tense situation that the key is lying in front of you but you do not notice it and go around asking everyone, where is the key? The car key is in your hand but you are unable to insert it in the slot - your hands are trembling! In such a situation, one is unable to see or hear properly. Such nervousness even leads to accidents. This is how you damage your hypothalamus with tension, and if the master computer is out of order, how can the processes function normally?

I have heard that a new airplane has been launched which doesn't need any human pilot, rather a sophisticated computer handles the flight. On its first test flight, the passengers were thrilled to get the chance to fly in such an advanced plane, which was being considered as a latest model of new space technology. The media gave it wide coverage, clicking photographs and asking the passengers for their comments.

Excited passengers were waving enthusiastically in front of the TV cameras, hoping their family members would catch a glimpse of them. Then the voice of the airhostess was heard: "Welcome to the technically advanced airplane. Please fasten your seat belts. The main doors of the plane are closing." Passengers looked around excitedly, an automated trolley came in followed by the announcement: "Orange juice, soft drinks, lemonade - please help yourself."

Everyone was surprised, for till now they were used to being served by an airhostess with whom they could communicate. But here there was no human being! The trolley came in on its own and made announcements. It stopped automatically at each seat, and only moved on when the passenger picked up a drink! Now, you may hesitate to pick up another drink when airhostess is offering, but here there were no restrictions. As soon as you picked up a drink, the snacks tray came up. The passengers were thrilled!

In the meanwhile another announcement was made: "The plane is ready to take off and you are all welcome on its maiden flight." Plane started moving towards runway to take off. As it taxied on the runway, the passengers started screaming with joy. There was not a single human being operating the plane; it was all automatic! Soon another announcement came: "Very soon we will fly high, touching the sky… grrr grr grr…" The plane got stuck on the runway and the announcement was going on: "fly high, fly high, fly high….and now the plane is airborne." All the passengers had the shock of their life!

If you are tense and stressed out, the computer that runs your body can develop a glitch. It doesn't matter what the cause of tension is, but this tension can cause a cerebral stroke in a second. It can also lead to heart attack or kidney failure or the blood pressure may rise so high that the blood vessels get severely damaged. It takes just a second for a blood vessel to burst, but the effect of such a stroke can be disastrous - like loss of speech - the portion of the brain that suffers the stroke will cause the functions of that area to be paralyzed like loss of vision or hearing ability.

Everybody thinks that such a catastrophe can happen to others and not to oneself, and that is why most of the people don't worry about their blood pressure. We worry a great deal about other things, but tend to neglect the blood pressure. Let me repeat that blood pressure might not have any physical symptoms. That is why you often hear it said about someone's death: "What happened! He was fine. What happened to him?" You thought he was fine because he looked fine. But what is the guarantee that he was fine inside too? When there are no symptoms, it is even more difficult to realise what's wrong inside the body.

Avoiding Hypertension

Now the question arises – How can a layman know or understand the importance of regulating the blood pressure? The ill effects of blood pressure are witnessed by all but what are its causes; the need to control it and how to do so – if you are not even thinking on these lines then it is certainly a cause of worry.

It is interesting that when we received applications for a meditation retreat, I was informed that most of the participants were over 40 yrs of age. Surprisingly, an international survey shows that these days most patients of high blood pressure are young - in the age group of 20 to 40 yrs. So, the ones who are suffering the most have presumed that they do not have blood pressure. And those above 40 yrs say that they control it with medication.

So, where is the need to understand, what it is, why it happens and how to control it? Just pop a pill and get along with your life seems to be the prevalent attitude. A doctor can only prescribe medication, but this has side effects.

For now we will talk about what we can do in order to keep the hypothalamus, which runs our body, in good health. This is a serious yet profound topic. You will hear some new terms – don't be amazed as I am not talking about an alien or unknown entity, but your own body and its parts.

Once I was conversing with some people in English. A lady - perhaps she was sitting far away or perhaps she was not well versed in English - was listening to us and did not understand the term 'hypothalamus'. She heard 'hippopotamus'! So she went home and told everyone that Gurumaa says there is a hippopotamus in our brain that controls our entire body!

The brain is protected by a thick bony structure called skull. The more precious the thing, the greater is the requirement for its security. The human skull is so strong, that at the time of cremation, the Hindus perform a rite in which the skull is burst opened by hitting it with a wooden staff. In spite of the high temperature of the pyre, the skull does not burst open. Have you ever wondered why this rite is necessary? One reason is to ensure that the skull is fully cremated and there is no residue. The son usually performs this skull-breaking rite. I feel it is a symbolic statement by the son saying: "Don't repeat these mistakes in your next life." In school, if you didn't learn your tables, the teacher would give you the best of ten cane hits on the palm and ten on the back of the hand. In the same fashion, the son performs the skull-breaking rite to imply that now that you have wasted this life, don't waste the next.

Mantra Sadhana, Sound Vibrations & Yoga Nidra

Let us see if we can aid our brain to function in a healthy manner. Most definitely we can! And the two best methods are mantra sadhana and yoga nidra. When you recite a mantra, sound vibrations are generated which have a direct effect on the brain. Sound vibrations can even break stones. Just as the powerful laser rays can break apart the gallstones, the sound waves can shatter solid materials.

There is a folklore that once a competition was held between Tansen and Baiju Bawara – musical legends. It was announced that the one who could shatter a piece of marble with his vocal vibrations - not with a hammer and chisel, not with an axe or spade, but with the sound vibrations produced by the vocal chords – would be the winner! It is said that Baiju Bawara succeeded and was declared the winner.

In Italian orchestra, they usually have a singer, generally female, who has a wide vocal range, who is called a 'Soprano'. They sing at a very high pitch, so much so that the sound can shatter a goblet kept in front!

Sound vibrations generate tremendous force and energy. When you recite a mantra, the sound vibrations produced have a direct impact on the hypothalamus, pituitary and pineal gland. Especially when you hum the sound of mantra with closed ears (to shut out all external sounds), the vibrations of that mantra reach your brain directly and change its frequency.

Medical science has no cure for the causes of hypertension, and the greatest cause of hypertension is tension! Is there any pill which can prevent tension? Not so far! So far all the medicines which are available, or being researched, can only cure the miserable symptoms occurring in the body due to tension. These hypertension pills are essentially chemicals - some are in the form of calcium tablets, some have the medicinal property to ease the pressure of the blood on the vessels, and some are blood thinners - they are anti-coagulants.

Medical science has no such pill that can prevent tension – but rishis have it and their pill is mantra. The mantra sadhana is not to please the invisible God, and in my view mantra recitation is not only a spiritual practice – mantra sadhana is in fact the most beneficial method to keep your mind, body and brain in perfect harmony.

I would like to emphasise that the vibrations produced by mantra sadhana bring immense transformation in the body - hypothalamus functions at its optimum and so do all other glands. And when all is well with the brain, then all is well with the parts below the brain – the power of mantra makes you healthy. So when you wake up in the brahmamuhurta to do mantra sadhana, know that you are making your body healthy.

"Guruji has given the mantra and instructed to chant daily", that's why I am doing it - get rid of this false notion! Your practice of the mantra does not benefit the guru in anyway; nor does your abstaining harm him in anyway. When you chant the mantra regularly, you benefit only your own self. You help your body to stay healthy, your mind free from stress and induce beauty and wellness in your life. And if you are not practicing it regularly, then you are not only mismanaging your body-mind system but also enhancing your vulnerability to stress related diseases.

Now we come to the same question - so what if the blood pressure rises? Remember, it can cause heart failure, brain haemorrhage, disability of speech, loss of vision, paralysis, kidney failure, anything can happen. And don't be under the impression that this disease happens only to older people, as these days it is even seen in the age group of 20 to 40 yrs. And the most important fact is that in many patients, there are no visible symptoms.

Suppose someday, by chance, you check your blood pressure and find it high and you also happen to have a headache, you would immediately relate the headache to the raised blood pressure. Whereas the headache could be due to some other causes like migraine, lack of sleep or may be the tension – tension is the biggest cause of headache. Or your ego is hurt by someone and you are agitated which is causing you headache.

Are you aware of the fact that constipation too can cause headache? You might wonder how the two are related – well, they are deeply connected. For example, if your kitchen bin is full and you keep adding garbage to it, and do not dispose it off, do not empty it - then particularly in the summer - it will begin to stink. If you still continue to fill it with garbage, the stink will go on increasing to the extent that it can cause a person to faint and collapse.

You may have read the news about municipal workers who died due to the toxic fumes emanating from the sewer that they opened for cleaning. The deadly gases produced by the human dung that goes in the sewer pipes can be so poisonous that it can kill a human being. Recently three such cases have happened in this manner – sewage workers went to clean the sewers and died right there. No one assaulted them, or killed them. So how did they die? They died because of the toxic fumes. Now the same process takes place in our body. When the faecal matter rots in large intestine, it gives rise to toxic fumes causing headaches, nausea, anxiety, and vomiting.

I have seen many people who are not bothered by a lack of bowel movement. Even after two days of lapse they remain unperturbed; on the third day they may consider that they need to do something about it. The food that is not ingested well remains stuck, and on top of it you go on eating more and more food. Every four hours you need tea or coffee or some beverage. If your system is not functioning properly, then beverages like tea and coffee will further aid into indigestion and constipation.

It is like setting the faeces in concrete and ensuring it never gets relieved. Longer the excreta remains in the intestines, the more it rots, giving rise to toxic fumes, which destroy the entire elimination process and also affect the digestive system. It also increases the acidic secretions in the stomach causing reflux and dyspepsia. Head begins to ache and recurring headache makes you feel that you have high blood pressure.

High blood pressure may give you dizzy spells, but it is not directly related to headaches. It can cause dizziness but not the headache; dizziness too may be due to a number of other reasons. High blood pressure is asymptomatic. It is advised to monitor blood pressure, but one should not be obsessed with checking it day and night.

Know Your Body

Understanding the processes of your body should be your primary responsibility. And it is also important to know how we can independently handle the problems that body may encounter. The most important cause of problems is tension and stress. It is stress that unsettles the entire system of the body – to counter this, mantra sadhana is an extremely powerful and beneficial tool.

CHAPTER 3

Adverse Effect of Lifestyle on Health

It comes as a shock when school going children commit suicide. They come under such intense stress that life seems meaningless to them. Man lives in a strange denial - when he witnesses the worst possible situations, he convinces himself that it will never happen to him or his children.

Just think: Did the parents of children, who commit suicide, ever imagine that their children would do something like this? Life is like a very delicate thread – its foundation is shaky. And only people with a strong foundation can win the battle of life – the foundation should not be weak. Now, who is responsible for a weak foundation? Teachers, parents, schools and families – no one teaches a child the value of life and what is most important in life that one should strive for. A child is only taught - "Grow up fast and earn lots of money" – as though earning money is the ultimate aim of life!

At home, when the parents talk about a relative or a well-known person, they refer to him in terms of his wealth and influence. The child absorbs the same values as he observes his parents. If a wealthy person visits home, the parents welcome him with reverence, fawning over him. And if a poor relative visits, you make do with whatever is cooked and no extra effort is made to welcome him, rather you wonder when he will leave. If the child spends too much money or demands expensive stuff – an expensive car or scooter, the parents may tell him that money is earned with a lot of struggle. At that point no one will say that 'money is everything'. Yet, each successive generation is becoming more selfish, ambitious and self-serving than the previous and your future generations will be even more so.

Most of the people have an overtly materialistic mentality and in order to compete with others they lose precious time in making more and more money. But while you are busy earning more money, what you lose is the invaluable time. Your forefathers worked hard to earn money and built the property, which you are enjoying. You think it is a tradition that parents earn and children enjoy the fruits of their endeavour; just as you are working for your children. All sounds very well! Not a bad idea; but, do not fall into the trap of working so hard that you suffer from ill health, and then treat yourself with medicines, the side effects of which lead to ten new diseases, and you end up simply filling the coffers of the doctors and chemists on a regular basis. Think why you are working so hard - for your doctor, or your chemist?

Today society is bearing the brunt of unknown and unwarranted stress. As I mentioned earlier, it is possible that blood pressure may rise without any visible symptoms, and you realise it only when you land up in a hospital. Have you ever met a person who has suffered a heart attack or a brain stroke? If you have not, do try to meet such a person and ask him - what he was doing at that time. He would not have imagined in his wildest dreams that this will ever happen to him. He may say that it happened all of a sudden; but remember, nothing happens all of a sudden. Slowly the disease festers, but mostly remains asymptomatic and non-specific symptoms like headache or dizziness which could have been the warning signals are ignored.

Side Effects of Medication

These days, hypertension is a great cause of concern as it is affecting younger people in the age group of 20 to 40 yrs. Even more worrying are the medicines that are prescribed to control hypertension; the more advanced the medicine is, the more detrimental are its side effects. The most commonly prescribed drugs are Diuretics – drugs that remove water from the body by causing excessive urination, thereby depleting the body of salts. As a result, the blood pressure comes down to normal, but once started, the medication has to be maintained. Adverse effects of these medicines cause severe harm to the kidneys.

Our body has essential electrolytes, which are depleted by excessive urination. By medication the blood pressure is normalised but prolonged medication damages the kidneys. If you treat your ailment properly, further possibility of disease can be subsided. So far I have suggested only one cure – mantra sadhana. Mantra sadhana requires no chemist, doctor, drug store, or any expenditure. You just need to find some time for yourself and practice the mantra recitation to keep your body healthy. Now tell me, isn't this a better treatment? Or would you rather take medication and destroy your electrolyte balance and damage your kidneys? So, think carefully before you start medication!

Another option given by physicians is 'beta blockers', which lower the heart rate. The function of the heart is to pump blood, and this medication reduces the heart rate, to lower the blood pressure – lower the speed of the pump, lower will be the blood pressure. But beta blockers too have side effects, for example nightmares which lead to excessive sweating and increased heart rate which had been lowered with medication. The heart rate now increases four fold. In addition to this, the resultant fear causes secretions of chemicals, which are extremely harmful for the body.

Third type of medication for hypertension is Methyldopa; this too lowers the heart rate. It acts directly on the heart. Its side effect is drowsiness – take the pill and fall asleep. You will keep feeling drowsy which leads to further lethargy. It also causes loss of libido in men, so the newly married ones or those who find pleasure in their married life should abstain from this medicine. Thus, this drug affects your heart and mind, induces sleep and its side effect is depression. Depression is when you feel miserable without any reason; life appears meaningless, even while living in all comforts and with the family, and you don't like to be in anyone's company. The extreme form of depression leads to committing suicide – the person just wants to end his life.

If we go deeply into the subject, then it can be said that the medication for high blood pressure gives rise to even more diseases, which not only harm your physical body, but also disturb your mental health. Therefore, those who feel that there is no problem and all is well because they are taking medicine for blood pressure - should think about it seriously.

Another drug that is prescribed by the doctors is 'Peripheral vasodilator', which acts on the diameter of the blood vessels. Just as water flows easily from a wider tube or pipe than from a narrower one, similarly, this drug works on the diameter of the vessel which affects the flow of blood. However, these too have unpleasant side effects like palpitations, headache and dizziness because you are playing around with nature! To cure one disease you are causing another one.

Mullah Nasruddin's son came back crying from school. His mother asked, "What happened son?", "I have not done well in school. I have got very low grades. Now father will thrash me", he said. "Don't worry", the mother consoled him. "I will have a word with him." The child was keen on studying, but he was upset at his poor grades and equally concerned about the thrashing he was about to receive. Mullah overheard this conversation and without a thought started beating the boy. The boy was surprised for he had not yet spoken to his father. Mullah said, "You have broken the vase in my room, our precious heirloom!" "No, I did not break it", the son pleaded. "Yes, you did", screamed Mullah.

This exemplifies how you create bigger misery to avoid smaller one! Similarly, you create severe ailment to cure the minor one! Now will you accept an even bigger disease to handle this situation? Hypertension is the symptom of a disease, not a disease. If it were a disease, we had the cause for concern. But if we address the causes of hypertension and attempt to treat them, it will automatically be cured. I would like to repeat that medicines only treat the symptoms and not the underlying cause.

It is like you have a termite-ridden tree in your garden and you go on cleaning and polishing the leaves everyday. You decorate it with artificial leaves and flowers and light bulbs to make it appear beautiful! Oh no! You must treat the termites, which are killing the tree. By artificial decorations you cannot rid the tree of termites. Similarly, as long as you do not treat the causes of high blood pressure, medicines may give you temporary relief, but the side effects of drugs will play havoc with your health and will further aggravate the situation.

Another group of drugs used in the treatment is 'Calcium channel blockers'. These drugs soften the muscles - the heart too is but a muscle.

The side effects of these drugs are unimaginable - they can have an adverse effect on the coronary arteries!

Sedatives are prescribed to put brain to sleep. The effort is to put the brain that is tense, worried, reactive and negative to sleep. Let it sleep, let it rest, but for how long? What happens when you wake up? You do need to wake up to eat, to work and to make arrangements for living. To put it simply, you can't get rid of your troubles by falling asleep.

Once I met a lady in Delhi who had not slept for several years after her husband's death. Her grief, tension and worries had overpowered her to an extent that to treat her blood pressure and make her sleep, sedatives were prescribed. As the normal dosage could not make her fall asleep, the dosage was increased. Gradually, the pills became ineffective and injections were given to induce sleep. Now she was able to sleep only after being injected, otherwise she just could not sleep.

She had come to attend my satsang where I conducted two sessions of meditation. On the fourth day, she presented me with a huge bouquet of flowers and said that she had slept the previous night. I wondered what was special about that – everyone sleeps at night! She said, "Since the past eight years I have been dependent upon sedatives for sleep but pills could make me sleep only for 4 hours and tranquilisers for 6 hours and because of abnormal blood pressure even this sleep was temporary. For the first time in several years, after meditation I just laid down and fell off to sleep last night, without any pills or injections. It was only in the morning when I woke up that I realised I had slept through the night without any pill. I checked with my son, who said, "I came to give you the injection but on seeing you asleep I presumed that you had already taken some medication. So I covered you with a blanket, switched off the lights and left the room." When I told him that I had not taken any medication at night, he could not believe his ears."

Change Your Lifestyle

The modern lifestyle of hurry, curry and worry is the main culprit leading to abnormal blood pressure. The eating habits are erratic and indiscriminate like eating food rich in saturated fats and refined sugar, eating at the wrong time and eating unconsciously, not even being aware of what you are eating. The food we eat constitutes our body and keeps our brain working. It also produces energy which is used for the functioning of the brain and mind. So what type of body do you want - unhealthy, lethargic, ailing? Keep this in mind that every time you eat stale food, you make your physical and mental self unhealthy.

Wonder, what would have been the idea behind inventing the refrigerator? The way it is used today is worth noticing. Just heat the refrigerated stale food in a microwave oven and eat it! Are you aware that when the oil in which food is cooked, is heated over and over, it leads to food degeneration.

Earlier generations did not have refrigerators and hence cooked fresh food every day. With the coming of the fridge, things have become easier – cook once and eat for long! Do you ever think - the less fresh food is, the more it is teeming with bacteria and microbes; the more often oil is reused and reheated, the more toxic and unhealthy it becomes.

Salt enhances the flavour of food - so you tend to eat excess of it, often adding salt on the table to already cooked food. Table salt is extremely harmful. This is the reason why the older generation still uses rock salt which is also commonly known as 'Pakistani salt'. Packaged salt is good to look at, but modern medical science calls it a white poison. Both, refined sugar and salt, according to them are poisonous. And how you relish both! I have seen many people just casually flick salt into their mouths! What enmity do such people have with their life? What grave injustice has life inflicted on them that they are ruining their body this way?

Your diet plays a vital role in the constitution of your body. Lifestyle can be a major contributor to the causes of vasoconstriction and therefore of high blood pressure; this includes eating frequently, overeating and eating too much salt. How often do you eat? Some people have a glass of juice before their meal and a sweet dish after! They feel a meal is incomplete otherwise! And then again in an hour and a half, they happily have a samosa, or some namkin or tea - means every two hours they need something to eat!

The abundance of wealth has got you the plentiful resources in life; but it should have also enhanced your patience – with the increase in money, your material possessions have increased but your sensibility has diminished. Now such foolish people go on satisfying themselves by eating - eating at odd times, uncontrolled eating and frequent eating causes vasoconstriction.

Impure blood is supplied by the heart to the lungs where it is oxygenated and returned to the heart from where it is then circulated to the entire body. If the vessels carrying the blood are constricted or narrowed, it is obvious that this will affect the blood pressure. It is also true that until we become aware of these facts, we cannot be expected to act on them. Usually, people relish eating at any time, any place. It will be a surprise if people pursuing such pleasures are not falling prey to diseases, and if they are diseased then it is not at all a surprise.

There should be a discipline in life for waking up, sleeping, and meal timings. Why? Firstly, most of the people wake up late in the morning because they go to bed late at night. Now, why do they sleep late? The reasons for sleeping late are varied: making money, scheming to make money, business meetings, guests and relatives – and if nothing else, then the great television set is always there; sometimes restlessness, worries and disappointments keep one awake.

Your body has important glands that produce hormones, which keep your body going. These glands are most active when the body is at rest; when you are sleeping. Where are these glands located? I have already mentioned about the three glands: hypothalamus, pituitary and the pineal are in the brain; thyroid and parathyroid are in the region of the throat; the adrenals are in the abdomen; hormones are also secreted from ovaries in women and testes in men.

There are several smaller glands in the abdomen, but we will address only the main six. It is the hormone secretions of these glands that govern our entire body and control our system. Now at the time when these glands are supposed to be active and producing vital hormones - you may be in a party enjoying yourself, chatting on the phone, browsing internet, or watching television; but your natural body systems and functions are undergoing a trauma because you are awake when you should be asleep and resting. And when the hormone secretion is depleted, it is but natural that your entire system will become dysfunctional.

Earlier I talked about getting up early, before sunrise, bathing and paying obeisance to the sun god. It is good if you pay salutations with suryanamaskara, and in case you don't know the right way to do suryanamaskara then you can offer water to Surya Deva while chanting the gayatri mantra and mantras like 'Adityaya Namaha'. This is extremely beneficial as the rays of the sun - ten minutes prior to and ten minutes after sunrise - are potent in ridding us of diseases and in keeping us healthy; healthy body and long life are the rewards of rising early.

Morning is the best time to work on your health. How? By practicing asanas, pranayama and suryanamaskara. But the moment I say asana, you begin to think about difficult asanas like shirshasana, mayurasana, ashtavakrasana and immediately reject the idea as not appropriate for you. Well, you get frightened lest your bones will get fractured. Maybe you did not get an opportunity to train yourself in your youth; school was a burden of books devoid of true learning; college presented books but not knowledge. A life bereft of learning and knowledge never blossoms, is never blissful. So your day should always start with asanas.

Primarily there are 36 joints in your body. These are kept supple by sukshma vyayama, which helps keep them free of pain and stiffness. If you want your car to keep working for long, you need to get it serviced regularly - I would like to ask you – when do you get your body serviced? Someone said they get their ECG and cholesterol checked once a year. That's fine! But the tests may reveal that your cholesterol is raised and then your doctor will hand you a prescription to buy medicines, whereas I want you to use your hard earned money in benevolent deeds and philanthropy – not on medicines. If you choose to spend your wealth on medicines, then do remember, we just talked about medicines and their side effects.

It is almost like you have a disease, you take medicine, and another disease comes free with it! A comb with a shampoo; a toothbrush with toothpaste! Similarly, along with the medicines of blood pressure you get six free diseases, and just to get more freebies, people buy more! What if your medication literature said you will be happy to take this medicine because it increases your depression, causes insomnia and kidney failure? No pharmaceutical company mentions, 'take medication only if very necessary, but don't get dependant on it'.

If someone who has neglected his health for long develops high blood pressure, he cannot be made to wake up early in the morning and start doing asana at that stage – he will have to resort to medication. While discussing blood pressure, I mentioned about vasoconstriction. Sometimes, it is possible, that due to some complication in pregnancy, the foetus developing in the mother's womb is born with narrow and constricted blood vessels, but such cases are rare. Bad eating habits are the prime reason for deranged lipid profile. All the fat and grease in your food raises the LDL (Low-density lipoprotein) and lowers the HDL (High-density lipoprotein) levels and causes the blood to become more viscous. Over a period of time, if dietary habits are not corrected, the cholesterol deposits in the arteries cause them to harden and narrow down.

Be warned that medicines in today's medical science can palliate but cannot cure any disease. Your body is a great blessing and gift from nature, and your priority should be to take proper care of it. Money is important, but only if you remain alive. What good is money if you are dead? Will you use currency notes instead of firewood for your cremation? Money is of use only while you are alive. I want you to live long, live healthy and utilise your wealth immensely. But first take charge of your body and health.

It is unhealthy to sleep late, for he who sleeps late wakes up late and is deprived of the bliss and benefits of the early morning. He not only loses the best opportunity to do yoga but also the benefits of early morning sunrays; a precious life is wasted and one is left with an ailing disease-ridden body. Let me reiterate that diseases do not occur overnight, they take time to develop.

At one time it was believed that only the affluent people suffer heart attacks. This notion was so much prevalent that society even wondered how anyone who is not wealthy could have a heart attack! Another misconception has been that only the elderly – those above 60 years of age - suffer from blood pressure. Ironically, today people as young as 20 years are afflicted with high blood pressure – it is even considered fashionable!

I remember a person asking his maid why she was absent the previous day. She replied that her blood pressure had gone low.
"Who said so?" he asked.
"The doctor", she replied.

"Was it high or low?" he asked.

"Whether high or low, I don't know, but there was something." she replied.

It seems as if being afflicted with high or low blood pressure has become a status symbol!

Any increase or decrease in blood pressure indicates that you are leading an undisciplined life. Had this not been the case, there is no reason to have blood pressure. Nature has made our body in such a way that it is intrinsically disease-resistant. As I mentioned earlier, human body can live for 500 yrs, if you live a controlled and disciplined life; eating the wrong food at the wrong time causes disease. Some people even feel that they will fall ill if they do not eat ghee! Who said that one falls ill for not taking ghee!

There is no harm in eating ghee, provided you fulfil a condition: you must walk 5-6 kms or jog 2 to 3 miles every day; or else, dismiss all your domestic help and do all the household chores – sweeping, mopping, cleaning utensils, washing clothes, shopping, changing the gas cylinder, cooking – do everything yourself. And be thrilled to receive visitors: 'Aha! Guests have arrived to help me keep fit and healthy.' It has been a culture in India to welcome guests as God, popularly known as 'atithi devo bhava', but cooking for guests seems an additional burden to you.

An undisciplined lifestyle leads to disease. If you live a disciplined life, it is possible to stay healthy and completely disease-free.

Ways to Lead a Healthy Life

Now let me tell you about the various ways to keep the blood pressure normal. The first method worth adopting is mantra sadhana. The strong and powerful vibrations of mantras have a profound effect on the entire body, and the mind too is calmed and stilled; you benefit not only physically, but also spiritually. Then why deny yourself this advantage?

The second method is yoga asanas. Asanas are beneficial only if practiced correctly. You are fortunate that here in the ashram you have an opportunity to learn yoga that is taught in a manner that makes it a pleasant experience and not a burden. If you practice the asanas correctly and regularly, soon you will become self-reliant with effulgent glow and a healthy body.

Understand it properly that 'may you live long' is not a blessing, but a resolve. The rishi blesses and ratifies the resolve of the human being when he says to the seeker that "May the resolve that you are instilling in your chitta be fulfilled." The rishi is not saying, "You will live long because I say so" - many people think that the 'live long' blessing of the mahatma will endow them with long life and so they go around seeking the blessings. But only the blessing of a long life will not prolong your lifespan. And if you follow the practices that are taught and prescribed to you and take a resolve at sunrise, then from today you will live for a hundred years.

In the next session, some more asanas like shashankasana will be added to the pavanmuktasana series taught today. The postures of these asanas will have a particular effect on the adrenal and brain glands, strengthening and normalising their function. Once they are normalised, all organs and parts automatically begin to function normally. In these series of asanas, you will also be taught yoga mudra and matsyasana – both, children and elderly people can do them easily. They cause no stress or strain, yet you receive their full benefits.

Along with pranayama, it is important to practice shatkarmas as well in which neti and varisara dhauti (shankha prakshalana) are extremely beneficial. I will discuss them in detail later. In brief, these are the two main techniques of shatkarmas to eliminate the toxins built up in your body. While neti cleanses the nostrils, sinuses, eyes, ears, and throat, varisara dhauti (shankha prakshalana) or intestinal wash detoxifies and cleanses the entire gastro-intestinal tract. If you have constipation then it will certainly cause no less than twenty other diseases. So it is vital for the digestive system to function properly – and these techniques help a great deal in maintaining the system in normal state.

Next is yoga nidra, which gives us physical, mental, emotional and intellectual rest. If you practice yoga nidra besides your mantra sadhana, asanas and pranayama, then you will be surprised to notice that even your constricted arteries will become normal. How? Well, this is the miracle of pranic energy. We kindle the pranic energy which gave rise to the existence of our body. How's your body formed? From the time of conception, till the time of birth, all development takes place with the energy of prana. Without pranic energy you would not have a body. Prana is not visible to the eye though, but it runs your body and its functions.

Blinking of the eyelids, hiccups, yawning and stretching, burping - all are happening through pranic energy. Digestion of imbibed food, throbbing of heart, blood-circulation are also powered by prana. Therefore, prana is the energy that formed this body, brought it into existence, and now is running it too. With the combination of pranayama, asanas, yoga nidra, mantra sadhana and shatkarmas, we can awaken and increase the latent pranic energy in our body, which helps keep it healthy and disease-free. Here in the ashram, you will not only learn all these, but as you practice them you will experience the transformative results at first hand.

I appreciate that all of you have realised your responsibility of this human life. And to keep your body healthy, hale and hearty, you have come here to acquire the knowledge required to do so. Otherwise, most people are not even aware of their responsibility and in their ignorance they leave everything to fate. And in the wake of this ignorance, they are not even aware of the rut they are trapped in. Situation is such that every day man himself feeds the cause of his ignorance, without even realising how it destroys his precious life and body.

Now, to do mantra sadhana, sit straight keeping the spine erect. Gently close your eyes and concentrate on your breath. Watch the gentle, natural flow of your breath as you exhale and inhale. Slowly take deeper breaths, keep the body still, do not move, and keep the hands, feet and fingers still i.e. 'kaya sthiram'. Take a deep breath... deeper, deeper, and deeper; increase the duration and depth of your breath keeping in mind that your breathing should not be audible.

When you are asked to 'breathe deeply', you do deepen your breath but it involves an effort which gives rise to a sound - this should not be so. There should be no sound; sit peacefully and quietly. Your breathing should be deep and long, but quiet and peaceful. Observe the entire passage of the breath carefully as it comes in and as it goes out. On inhalation, the chest and stomach expand slightly – be aware of every little activity, concentrate on all that happens in the body when you breathe.

Take a deep breath, and now while exhaling, chant OM. A-U-M: the confluence of these three gives rise to OM. Coincidently, your brain also has only three glands: hypothalamus, pituitary and pineal. OM is formed by three sounds and brain too constitutes of three glands. So begin with a loud recitation of OM and slowly lower the volume till you are silent. Then proceed to a mental recitation of OM – you are now ready to advance to the final stage i.e. gunjan of OM (the humming of OM).

At the time of gunjan, shut your ears with the index fingers, or form yoga mudra – this will be profoundly beneficial. When you are humming OM mantra, your focus and attention should be on your cerebrum, head and forehead. This activates the dormant neurons, as the sound vibrations of the mantra reach the finest neurons in the brain. If your master computer i.e. brain is fine, your entire body is healthy and synchronized.

Mantra sadhana practiced in this manner is God's worship as well as a means to a healthy body. Therefore, whenever you do the gunjan of OM, realise that you are purifying your body which embodies the lord's temple. Just as the temple made of bricks and mortar is cleaned with a broom, the temple of body is cleaned and energised by the vibrations of OM. It will add lustre to your lustreless faces and make them glow with radiance.

CHAPTER 4

Importance of Dental Hygiene

If your oral hygiene is poor and your gums are unhealthy, then you are at the risk of heart disease. Now the question arises: How is this possible? When the gums get infected, the bacteria can enter the blood stream and reach the coronary arteries (supplying blood to the heart muscle), causing inflammation of these blood vessels. This in turn promotes building of plaque in the arteries with consequent hardening and narrowing of these arteries. This compromises the blood reaching the heart and leads to heart attack (medically known as ischaemic heart disease). Women have narrower blood vessels compared to men. Therefore, plaque deposits cause them greater harm as they make the blood vessels still narrower.

Sometimes when you get the ECG (Electrocardiography) done, you are thrilled to find it normal – it means all is well with you, and you suffer from no ailment. But an ECG is not a comprehensive and conclusive test. Every man and woman above the age of thirty should go for regular health check-ups without waiting to develop symptoms of any disease.

Indians love films. When a person is shown having a heart attack in a film, he screams and clutches his chest, sweating profusely he collapses to the ground. Anyone around him will have no doubt that he is having a heart attack. Although in 80% of the cases the indigestion and flatulence may also lead to stiffening of the jaw, severe chest pain and nervous tension, and it might not necessarily be a heart attack.

You must not have ever heard or imagined how deep the connection between the heart and the jaw is. The American Dental Society has declared that it is more important to keep your teeth and gums plaque free than to brush them. Dental floss – a type of special thread, is moved between the teeth, back and forth, to remove plaque. The toothbrush cleanses the external surfaces, but plaque remains hidden between the teeth. Women are more susceptible to plaque deposits because their blood vessels are narrower – this won't get detected by an ECG – therefore a blood test is essential. Understand one thing carefully: If ECG is normal, then it does not indicate that you have no heart disease; a blood test will make the picture clearer. For women, the LDL (Low-density lipoprotein) level is of great significance – it should not exceed 130 to 159 mg/DL.

Heart Disease: A Different Perspective for Men and Women

The male physiology differs from the female in the matter of coronary artery disease. If you want a clear picture of HDL (High-density lipoprotein), LDL (Low-density lipoprotein) and cholesterol, get a Lipid Profile Test done. It is important to check the level of LDL in women to see if there is any constriction in the arteries. If the LDL level is raised, then there is an increased risk of heart disease.

There was a time when more women suffered from heart disease than men; today the ratio is almost equal. If we look back 30 to 40 years, we will find that mothers and grandmothers did all the household chores themselves; domestic help and gadgets were rare. Today the household, especially the kitchen is ruled and run by gadgets and appliances. Prosperity does not bring convenience alone – it brings diseases too.

Earlier, mothers used to grind all spices and condiments by hand; the sensible ones would even ground the whole-spices by hand at home. Even for cooking food - onion, ginger and garlic were grounded in a mortar and pestle. During winters, poppy seeds and almonds were pasted by hand to make recipes for children. As soon as winters used to start, this routine too would start. This grinding procedure was so strenuous that the entire family would join in to help. If mother started the grinding, soon father would offer to relieve her so that she could attend to some other chore. In my childhood, we kids found it amusing to watch them grinding and soon we would join in. And then after an hour's effort, the almond and poppy seed milk would be ready to drink.

Besides all the work mothers would personally clean, winnow, wash the wheat and take it to the mill for grinding. They would soak, scrub, wash and rinse the linen themselves, besides attending to other jobs in the house. After so much hard work, whatever you eat gets easily digested. So, people who do physical labour are unlikely to have high cholesterol levels.

In those days very few people owned scooters, even fewer owned cars; cycles were the popular means of transportation and most people preferred to walk. Even to hail a tonga or rickshaw, you had to walk some distance. But now in this age of internet and technology, press the call bell and your servant will bring you tea! Before the coming of the remote control, you at least had to get up from your sofa, walk to the TV set, change the channel and then walk back. At least you got to move! Now you change a hundred channels sitting in one place. Man has become such a couch potato! He cannot move; he does not need to move; he does not need to cook – just pick up the phone and order in! Microwaves, mixer-grinders, refrigerators, and washing machines – all have freed you from the tedium of housework. Now there is a huge variety of frozen processed foods to choose from.

A few days ago I spoke to an eighty-five year old lady. Her lifestyle is such that she eats early dinner; she eats only one vegetable and even if you serve a second dish, she will not eat it. She rarely eats sweet – on a festival or at a wedding she may, but not every day.

Your diet has a deep impact on your health, especially on your heart. What to eat and what not to eat in a certain season – our ancestors were aware of this exposition from the ancient ayurvedic texts. So they had complete knowledge about seasonal fruits and vegetables, and never ate any non-seasonal, stale food or anything from the cold storage. Moreover they ate only moderately but did lot of physical labour – a style which you have never adopted; you live a very easy & comforting lifestyle.

At home, you just ring the bell and your servants serve you food, or you order a meal from any take away or home delivery joint and food is delivered. At the push of a button, all your work is done. This kind of sedentary lifestyle slowly, over a period of time, increases the fat in the body, raising the LDL levels and destroys the healthy balance. Soon the person lands up in a hospital! Even there you are given a remote! To call the nurse; to ask for food; if you are in pain, just press a button. Even there you are playing with a remote.

No sane person would want to fall ill, take medicines, and get admitted in a hospital or run after doctors. But the life you are leading almost ensures an enduring relationship with doctors and hospitals. Maybe that is why many parents are keen to marry their son/daughter to a doctor! A doctor in the family would be such a convenience! Well, if your daughter-in-law or son-in-law is a doctor, will you insist on having regular injections?

Expensive treatments, mental tension, wastage of time, and the biggest thing is that you are relinquishing the vitality of your life. What is the life of a sick person? He just lives by the prescription: 4 tablets in the morning, 2 in the afternoon, 1 before meals, 2 after meals, 1 at night to sleep well! Won't you take a pill to wake up? What if you remain sleeping? Sedatives for sleeping, digestives for digestion, purgatives for excretion – such a lifestyle is totally wrong. I have already told you that blood vessels are narrower in women – so after the age of thirty, they should definitely get their complete medical check-up done, to avoid any major health condition, and address it before it is too late. The test will also reveal the damage that you have done to your body by your undisciplined lifestyle. Visit the best pathology laboratory near you, and get a basic Lipid Profile Test and ECG done. If your cholesterol is normal and you do not have sugar, then there is nothing to worry. But if your blood sugar is high and your blood report is not normal, then you must visit your doctor at once. These tests are important to determine whether or not all is well with you.

You can improve the worsened situation to a certain extent only. In some cases, you just need to bring about a change in your lifestyle, dietary habits and sleeping pattern, and make meditation, concentration, mantra chanting and yoga nidra a regular part of your daily routine – this is sufficient to make you disease-free. There is no cause for worry, but before you change your lifestyle and adopt all these practices, it is good to have a basic knowledge of your situation, like women should be aware of their LDL and HDL levels.

Indiscipline is the Main Cause of Diseases

The main reason for the diseases to occur in the body is your undisciplined mind. For example, according to ayurveda, you should not overeat; in fact it is recommended that you eat only that much which satiates half of your hunger. But you go on eating immodestly, till your stomach is ready to explode because of overeating, especially if the dish is to your liking. I have mentioned earlier also that wealth has given you power and freedom – to buy anything, to eat anything - but mind it that senseless and indiscriminate overeating leads to a number of health problems like diabetes, hypertension and heart attack.

If there is a congenital defect in the structure of the heart, then of course it is not your fault. There are some children who are born with a hole in the heart – they are called blue babies – or their arteries are blocked since birth. It is very astonishing to know about this and one is struck with wonder as to how is this possible.

One can understand that a hole in the heart may be due to a structural defect – even though the parents would say that it is not their fault and would lay the blame on nature. However, according to Rishi Parashara, the parents are to blame. You may wonder how is possible? This is so, as a child conceived at an inappropriate time can never be healthy. Whether you believe it or not, kala chakra has a deep and profound effect on your mind and body.

The night of the new moon - amavasya - is called the dark night. There are some days and festivals, mahurata and kala that should be spent doing austerity, meditation, prayer, japa and staying awake all night. But men and women driven by passion give in to the sexual urge. The child born of such a union is likely to be unfit – when I say unfit it includes both body and brain as these are very deeply connected. The brain governs the body and connecting the two, brain and body, is the nervous system. If the nervous system is dysfunctional, then the brain-body co-ordination is lost.

According to swara yoga, if a child is conceived when both the man and the woman are breathing through the left nostril – which is known as chandra swara – then the baby will be born handicapped. This is the science of life; it is not a matter of auspicious or inauspicious timings but it is science. In olden days, fishermen used to notice the wind and the sky, the intensity of waves and the tides, and in case there were tides in the sea, no fishermen would take his boat into water.

Now we get the information through satellites and fishermen are told about the days when not to go to sea – as the waves can be really high and there could be a possibility of storm too. Those who have ever vacationed by the sea must have noticed a flag posted on the shore. A red flag signifies danger and warns people not to go by the sea. This is not a matter of auspiciousness or inauspiciousness – it is sheer stupidity to venture further even when you can see danger right in front of you. So, one should go at a suitable time.

You will be very surprised to know that the revered scripture like Yoga Vasistha mentions that Rishi Vasistha, the family priest of the Ikshvaku dynasty, was an astrologer of great standing with in-depth knowledge of astronomy. Rishi Parashara was also an astrologer. You will wonder how is this related to our lives – well, there is a profound relation.

The sun and moon are closely connected with our health. That is why yogis and rishis of ancient times took a keen interest in an in-depth understanding of the movement and placement of the stars, planets and constellations, and how they affected our bodies. Even today, in the villages where there are no compasses or watches, people study the night sky and use those readings to navigate their travel in the day; such places still exist.

The body is not only constituted of five elements but is also run by them. Therefore, you cannot deny the effect of these five elements on the body. The solar energy of the sun powers the mechanisms of the body - you cannot deny this; the moon has a deep connection with the mind - you cannot deny this too. It's a different matter that people are not aware of this or don't understand this.

In Australia, a doctor learnt yoga and studied the scriptures from an Indian Guru. He also adopted and practiced the teachings very sincerely. In his research document, he mentioned that the percentage of patients coming to his hospital with complaints of migraine, spondylitis and frozen shoulder was higher around the time of the full moon. As the moon waned, he found that the patients coming in were reporting the descent of pain lower down in the body; by the time of the new moon, the pain in the lower back, legs and cases of varicose veins increased. He shared that at first he felt it was just a coincidence and did not pay any attention to it. But when he did, he realised that for the last four years this pattern was consistent in two of his hospitals: at full moon, there were more instances of head, eyes, nose, ears, face, neck, spondylitis and shoulder related problems; as the moon waned, the problems migrated downwards; by the time of the new moon, more patients reported feet and leg related problems. Since this is a research document of just one person and the doctors of medical research do not give much credence to the research of a single individual, I still feel this is a crucial piece of information relevant to all.

Parents' Role in the Health of the Child

The time, place, moment and breath pattern in which a child is conceived determines his body, mind and future – his whole life. If the mother's diet is deficient in nutrition, won't the child be sick?

When an expectant mother smokes, or her husband sitting close to her smokes, the smoke is transmitted into the body of the mother and through her body it gets transmitted into the body of the unborn child. The unborn child is exposed to smoke at a delicate and sensitive stage in its development – can it ever be healthy? If a woman has not taken an appropriate diet, the malnutrition is evident in her child. Won't her thoughts affect it too? Won't her feelings also affect the child?

Life is tough – it is not as easy as it seems. Your parents have a great contribution in making you what you are; your life is also greatly influenced by the emotional state of your parents when they brought you into this world. There is a startling stanza in the swara yoga text: "If the flow of breath through nostrils (swara) is not normal, or if the breath is flowing in a manner that has a lunar or cooling influence on the body, then a child conceived at such a moment will surely be born with some mental or physical deficiency." No one knows anything about this, no one talks about it and no one ever divulges it. Lucky are the people who acquire this knowledge; it is a different matter that they may or may not utilise or implement it, but even being able to know about this information is not a small achievement.

Getting back to our main topic, we discussed that the leading cause of heart disease is high blood pressure; another cause can be an anatomical defect. But as you are doing well right now, we can safely conclude that all is fine with you.

On the very first day of this camp, a lady walked up to me and said that six months ago she had had a sudden heart attack. First of all, please get rid of the word 'sudden' from your dictionary because nothing happens all of a sudden; disease takes time to develop. Therefore, it is imperative that you keep your body healthy and for that you need to keep an eye on your mind too. Hence, the primary cause of disease is inappropriate diet, the second is stress, and the third can be a congenital birth defect.

Women should be Extra Cautious

Women should remain more cautious as their blood vessels are narrow; they need to take extra care of themselves. It is generally said that the head of the family is the man, but I feel it is the woman – who makes the house a home, who takes on the responsibility to look after her husband, children and family. In my view, woman is the real head of the family, and not the man; man works to bring in the money, but it is the woman who runs the house - just because men have the physical strength to earn wealth, they are under the misconception that 'I am the head of the family'.

If a woman falls ill or dies suddenly, just imagine the state of her children! Not to worry about her husband - he will find another one very soon; men make these arrangements in advance – just as you keep a spare tyre in your vehicle! It is in the man's nature to look around, plan and fantasize. It is therefore even more important for a woman to take extra care of herself. I do not say that men should not look after themselves.

When Mullah Nasruddin's donkey died, he cried profusely. People wondered as he didn't grieve so much when his wife passed away, so why is he wailing so much on the death of a mere donkey. His neighbour asked, "Mullah, you didn't cry so much on the demise of your wife, then why are you crying like this now?" Mullah said, "My donkey was very dear to me and so was my wife. When my wife died, everyone said, "Do not cry Mullah, we will find you another wife." Now that my donkey has died, no one is offering to get me another. So, my donkey is more precious than my wife."

A woman should be more careful and cautious about her health because she is a mother and is responsible for the education and upbringing of her children. So, she needs to be extra alert to this fact.

Never be under the misconception that this disease can never afflict you. But if you lead a regulated life, sleep on time, remain stress free, walk at least three hours a week, do yoga every day, eat a healthy diet, practice yoga nidra daily and do your mantra japa regularly, then I can safely say that 99.99% you will not get a heart attack.

Those who live a disciplined life, those who live responsibly, do not suffer from heart disease. Diseases happen when you are irresponsible towards your own body; therefore, taking care of your body should be your primary duty. Because only with this body, sadhana can be done, world can be experienced, game of life can be played and all that you want to do can be done – to do all this, you need life. If there is no life, what can you do?

The lady who spoke to me about her heart attack also said, "Now I am always nervous and worried that I may get another attack, so I never leave from the house alone." This is called fear psychosis. When a deep-seated fear sets in as the result of an unpleasant experience, and you keep worrying that it may happen again, then unwittingly you are attracting it. In a way you are saying, 'Please come, I miss you' as you remember it every day.

Positive Attitude is Essential for Good Health

When you are careless and neglect your body, you fall ill. Now to avoid the disease from happening again, change your lifestyle and more importantly change your mindset. Your body is defined by your mindset; it is important to understand that what you think, sooner or later becomes the reality; what you imagine, will manifest. And this power is latent within all of you but you are unaware of it and don't know how to utilise it. Instead, you worry about an unknown future; you worry about sickness, become apprehensive about the recurrence of heart attack, and even death. In case you get to hear about someone of your age or younger dying, you become even more fearful. As a result of these fears, you become more depressed, and now this depression doesn't allow you to live a healthy life.

That is why I say that if modern man has to live a healthy and normal life, yoga nidra is a must. Just as you bathe every day to keep your body clean and you eat daily to keep your body healthy, similarly yoga nidra is a must for the replenishment of the mind – it removes the impurities of the mind. How does it do this? Let me give you an example. Suppose you ask your husband for something and he says he will get it in the evening. You say, "Do get it, don't forget." But all day you keep thinking that he is so forgetful he will surely not remember; after two hours you call to remind him. For the next four hours you continue to think of something or the other, maybe a relative you dislike is likely to visit. He has not yet arrived but you start remembering all the unpleasant memories associated with your relationship with him - this is stress, this is tension. If you apply for a job, promotion or transfer, you keep dwelling on it – whether or not you will get it, what will happen if you do and what will happen if you do not.

The mind keeps weaving a web of thoughts and you keep sinking in your self-created quagmire – is this not strange? The future is unknown yet, but by worrying about an uncertain future you ruin your present.

There are such beautiful clouds in the sky, cool and fresh breeze is blowing, the birds are chirping, butterflies are floating by, beautiful children passing by laughing and smiling…but you are totally unaware of all this. Why? Because you are so caught up in your own worries that you are completely disconnected from the nature and this present moment. You are constantly concerned about your mother-in-law's visit, your boss' visit, due payments, house to be bought and what not. You are so entangled in such mundane and baseless worries that you distance yourself from the beauty of the present; and then you wonder how to be happy.

If you keep on spinning the web of tension around you, then be warned, that even if God himself were to appear before you, you wouldn't even notice. People often ask "When will we meet God?" I say, stop worrying about that, instead worry about how to come out of the ignorance of unconscious thinking, for until you do so, you will not even see the world that is in front of you – then how do you hope to see God?

Tension is the Root Cause of all Diseases

You go on accumulating tension and this tension not only infests your mind but your body as well. Due to stressful thinking, the back of the shoulders become tense. Now the thought process goes on in the mind, but it affects the entire body. The shoulders get taut and a time comes when you may even develop knots in the shoulder muscles.

A good massage therapist can touch your muscles and tell how tense you are. Thoughts are in the mind, but the tension manifests as pain in the shoulders, neck, head and back. A hyper-tense person is more prone to flatulence, indigestion and acid reflux because of increased acid production. You take medication for head ache, back ache, stomach problems, but how do you hope to get well unless and until you address the root cause of all this – tension. Where is the root? The root of diseases is in the mind, and the effects are seen in the body. You have accumulated layers upon layers of tension and stress in your mind, body and chitta – yoga nidra can remove these layers.

How Yoga Nidra Cures

When you practice yoga nidra, and you reach the resting stage, you are asked to take your awareness slowly upwards from the toes to the soles of the feet, ankle, knees, thighs and further upwards. During this rotation of awareness, you must focus more on the area that has a particular problem, like stomach, shoulder, feet, legs, head, etc.

Suppose you have a painful shoulder; during yoga nidra, when I instruct you to be attentive of your shoulders, remain very alert and make the resolve that you are getting better and the pain is going away. Or else, just notice wherever there is pain or discomfort – just be aware of it, do not think about it – and when you move your awareness over your body, pay special attention to those parts. And at the time of making a resolution, if you choose to resolve for a healthy body, then give extra attention to the parts in pain. Now you might ask, how does this help?

Well, the mind that has caused disease by its negative thoughts can also bring forth cure by thinking positively. The potential of the mind is tremendous. A psychologist in USA University did an experiment - an extremely thin and weak man was convinced that he could lift a rock that was twice his weight. He was repeatedly suggested hypnotically into believing that he could do it – and he did it!

In another experiment, the man was asked to lift a rock that was half his body weight. But he was preconditioned into believing that he was not up to the task, that it was impossible for him to do so. He was told that they already knew that he could not do it. He was so discouraged, that when put to the task he could not even move the rock.

Mind over Matter

The mind is more powerful than matter. And in yoga nidra we awaken this very inherent power. It needs no therapist or guide - you become your own therapist and guide. You become your own saviour. You yourself lift the layers of tension to make your mind stress-free. Let your body loosen up and relax - relax every part of the body. Observe every part as a witness. Observe the entire body and move your awareness from head to toe and back from toe to head. Generally, you are unaware of your own body, but with yoga nidra you get well acquainted with it. And then while resting, the body gets so relaxed that when I instruct you into visualisation (in the end), its effects reach the deepest layers of your emotions.

When I take you on a mental journey where you visualise, you see the temple, the grass, the sky, the sun, the moon, the desert, the flowing water, and the beach - all in your mind. When you picture these scenes in your mind, your power of visualisation is greatly enhanced in yoga nidra.

This technique of visualisation is effective in the dispersal of various repressed tensions, painful experiences and traumas. Once I was conducting yoga nidra in England; after the session, a lady walked up to me and said that when I said 'beach', she was able to visualise a beach, but along with it she was reminded of an unpleasant experience. Once when she was holidaying in Spain with her family, they had all gone to the beach. It was all crowded when suddenly everyone stood up and started looking in a particular direction and running towards it. Seeing the crowd coming in her direction, she felt a terrible sensation of fear and suffocation, as though she was trapped. But as next instruction to visualise 'moon' came she said somehow a burden got lifted and now she feels much lighter as if a very painful burden has been lifted off.

Such agonising experiences create a very deep impression in subconscious and it becomes difficult to ever remove them from mind. These impressions can create such deep-rooted fears that a person can become hysterical. So when she visualised the beach, it brought up old memories and she started feeling the same sensations of fear, suffocation and claustrophobia. But when she went on to visualise the moon, all her unpleasant memories disappeared. And then, as she continued to watch the breath, there were some blockages that got dissolved and some mental hurdles that got removed.

To date, all the research that has been done on yoga nidra concludes that yoga nidra can cure all fears and phobias. For example, some people are scared of lizards, some are fearful of dark narrow places, where as some are daunted by heights, while some are frightened to use lifts and prefer to climb stairs instead – even this is curable with the help of yoga nidra. The more stress-free you become, the more the knots resulting from tension are unravelled.

With regular practice of yoga nidra, you can even cure yourself of allergies, which are usually suppressed with medication. Some people are allergic to flowers, perfumes, grass or silk. Some people are even allergic to milk! Well, how would one live if you are allergic to this and that - shut yourself in a glass chamber! You are a human being, try to live like one! But the list of allergens continues to grow. The cause of allergies is also in the mind and in your faulty lifestyles. With the practice of yoga nidra, you take over the reins of your body. As your body relaxes, your mind also begins to relax and your breath becomes cool, calm and deep – all these cures take place at different levels. Through yoga nidra, the roots of diseases are eliminated and you are prepared to stay calm in any distressing situation.

This is how yoga nidra helps you to prevent and cure many diseases. In my opinion, in this century - a century of stress - if you are not enlightened, then there is no other alternative for you to survive tension but this practice of yoga nidra. You may wonder why an enlightened one does not need yoga nidra. Because to him this world is a cosmic play, a game that he is witnessing, which is just like a dream. To him the truth is beyond this illusionary world and his mind always rests in peace, so he worries about nothing.

If you are a consummate devotee enthralled by God's love, then you too will not need yoga nidra. When there is no stress, why would you need a method of removing it?

Stay Calm in an Emergency

Whenever you are in a situation of great stress or nervousness, immediately start taking deep breaths. Close the mouth and breathe through the nose. Keep inhaling till the lungs are filled with air and the chest expands. Then exhale deeply. If you do this for 5-10 minutes, the situation may remain unchanged, but you will not be agitated anymore; you will be relieved from the state of tension you had put yourself in. Only if you are stress-free and calm can you face a situation with a clear head and find an intelligent solution. If you are nervous, you tend to make mistakes and even an obvious solution is missed.

A gentleman once told me this story: "It was a holiday and I was sitting at home reading a newspaper; the children were playing outside. Suddenly I heard my son wailing. He had fallen down and an iron object had pierced his stomach. As I ran out and saw him bleeding, I was so stunned that I could not move; I stood rooted to the spot. My wife urged me to move, to do something. With great difficulty I went downstairs and blanked out completely. I could not remember where my car or car keys were. My wife handed the keys to me and I sat in the car and came onto the road. Now I just could not remember the route to the hospital. It was as though my brain had stopped functioning. Somehow we reached the hospital and put the child on the stretcher. Seeing him bleed my tension peaked and I passed out. When I gained consciousness I found myself on a hospital bed with a glucose drip on! I was told that my son had a minor injury, nothing to worry about."

Now this gentleman did not stop for a reality check. He just saw that the child had fallen down, was injured and bleeding, and his brain just stopped working. He brought the child to the hospital but now the child is asking him if he is all right! The child is worried that he has such a faint-hearted father! He is not only faint-hearted; he is weak of mind too. He came under stress. He became frightened lest anything would happen to his child.

Fear often causes physical and mental freeze; do not allow your mind to panic. Try to remember that God makes this body and he is the one who runs it. Then why worry? What will your worry get you? If answer is nothing, then why worry?

When you are faced with a difficult situation or any trouble arises, it is even more imperative that you remain relaxed and don't become excited and agitated. I have seen many people reacting so dramatically to the slightest of troubles - they just start shouting, screaming and become unrelentingly anxious.

I would like to quote a small tale. This story happened some 30 years ago in Japan: Two cars collided; both the drivers came out. One bows to the other and says, "I am sorry, please forgive me. Should I drop you home?" The other bows to him and says, "Should I drop you home?" Both are asking each other - if he is hurt. One says, "Should I take your car to the garage?" "No, everything is all right." "Then at least accept some money." "My car is insured." "Sir please at least come and have tea with me this evening." Both are upset that they have damaged the car. But the one whose car is damaged is saying that he has insurance and in any case he has to buy a new car in 6 months. But this is an old story, these days things have changed there too. At a conference in Jaipur recently, one gentleman met me, who had come from Japan. He related a rather disturbing fact that young children there are committing suicide. He said to me that I should visit Japan as I was needed there.

Say if this accident had happened here on Delhi roads - if one car collided with another, the result would had been - shoes, fisticuffs, police, court – a good entertaining scene! Circumstances in life never remain same – every time there arises a new situation to deal with – we should handle them sensibly, like if your car has collided with another car and the other person too is very stress-free and you are also very calm - then you would just say, "Ok - Never Mind."

Why should you bother about minor scratches if you know how to make insurance claims? If you are dishonest and you know how to make false claim with help of your surveyor then too be stress-free, then too you need not worry. When an accident happens the damage is done, all you can do is have it fixed, so what is the point of getting into an argument or fight?

I have noticed something strange: if two cars collide, the drivers or owners get down and start fighting, and soon it won't be just the concerned parties fighting as passers-by would also join them - no matter how urgent an assignment they are on – they will also stop to see what is happening. A crowd would appear on the scene - one will relate the whole incident, another will ask, "Who is responsible?" So those who are fighting will receive one whack from him too. It has happened so - fight between two people attracted a crowd that later on turned violent and soon there was a riot; entire market was burnt down on a flimsy scuffle. What started it all? A cyclist collided with another cyclist, and shops were burnt, stones were pelted, people were injured, people were killed and ultimately the police had to resort to firing.

You are living with so many tensions and stresses - it is almost as though you are waiting for a provocation to explode, to break someone's head. Well, if you don't, someone else will give vent to his pent up feelings.

If you have understood what I have explained and if you practice yoga nidra regularly, then even if someone says something unpleasant to you or provokes you to fight, it is highly possible for you to remain so calm and controlled that this whole scene would begin to appear just like a film, which you are watching on a screen. During the practice of yoga nidra, if you take a resolve that 'no matter what the provocation be, I will never lose my mind', then no situation can ever incite you for a fight or an ugly scene. Thus, you become very calm and patient. So much so that you may even say, "Please, show me your angry expressions once more, they were marvellous!"

If you still feel anger or agitation arising in your mind, somehow at that moment you must pay attention to your breath and mentally recite OM. If this experiment succeeds once, you can remain assured that you are now ready to live a stress-free, anger-free and healthy life.

Realising the Wisdom

I am hopeful that if you regularly practice the methods I am teaching, you will experience a change in your life. And the day you experience this transformation, I will feel the time spent on you has been compensated, or else it will remain a debt on you.

According to the scriptures, you should serve the Guru and offer dakshina in return for the wisdom you receive - only then are you free of his debt - otherwise your debt towards the guru accumulates. Practice what you have been taught – that is the way to be free of the Guru's debt, this is true dakshina.

You often proclaim that you do not keep any debts, but here you are accumulating the debt of knowledge; the debt you owe me. How will you pay it off? The only way is to internalise this knowledge and make it a part of your daily life.

Always remember that anger and stress harm the incumbent and no one else. So, you have to keep them away; you have to protect and save yourself from them. Someone asked, how can he stay away from stress when stress is the other name of his wife? This gentleman has written, "Now I have understood what to do. As soon as I go home I will divorce her because as long as she is with me I cannot be stress-free." Well, if God forbid, you do have such a wife, I will say that you are a very lucky man, because you are halfway to being Socrates!

Socrates' wife was a very angry woman, always fighting with him and creating stress. His disciples often said: "Why don't you get rid of this trouble? She insults you, troubles you, and fights with you. She is so negative, full of dark qualities - a witch, why do you stay with her? Why don't you leave her?"

Socrates would reply, "She is very good the way she is, because as long as she is around I am undergoing a constant test - whether my mind is calm or not, she tests it; whether my mind is in equanimity or not – she shows it to me; and she also checks if any attachment has found place in my mind. You cannot imagine how kind she is to me and how indebted I am to her." So all the men whose wives are cruel and cunning are halfway to becoming Socrates.

And all the women whose husbands are cruel to them are just like wife of Hiranyakashipu - a demon king. Demons depicted in puranas do not have fangs, claws and horns - they had anger, aggression, ego and dark qualities. Hiranyakashipu's wife was a devotee of Vishnu - she sang his praises. So even though her husband was a demon, it did not affect her in the least bit.

We don't have to run away from a situation but to face it. We have to learn how to deal with it while living in it. Those who say that they can never find peace within their homes are not being sensible. Stop reacting to people around you, stop fighting with them - whatever they may be like, accept them as such. Now you have to see how good you are and how you can keep yourself calm and peaceful without losing control, without shouting and without being upset. This will be your real test and succeeding in this test would be your real achievement.

Let me reiterate this again that it is very important to understand your body and to manage your body in order to live a fulfilling, meaningful life.

CHAPTER 5

Heart of the Matter

The human body is nature's most beautiful and supreme creation. Each part of human body is a brilliant piece of architecture - the most interesting and enigmatic is the heart. It has captured the imagination of poets through the ages – from Kalidasa to Valmiki, from Shakespeare to modern day poets – all seem to be enamoured by the heart. The heart gets hurt, heart falls in love, it is sad, it is happy - this is a poet's vision and views about heart - but what is the heart? It is a unique instrument, made up of muscles, that works like a pump. It sends the impure blood to the lungs and circulates the purified blood to the entire body.

When our eyes are tired we shut them in order to give them some rest, feet are also given rest when tired, and even the digestive system is rested with fasting. Each and every part of our body needs relaxation and at sometime or the other we rest it. The brain too needs rest, which it gets when we sleep for six to seven hours. Thus, when the sense organs and limbs are tired, they can be rested. But we never rest the heart! Because if the heart rests, you will rest forever! If the heartbeat stops, that will be the end of the body.

Have you ever checked whether or not you have a heart? Or are you going around without one! Jokes apart, we are all born with a heart which beats in our chest cavity. The heart normally beats 70 to 80 times a minute and in some cases this figure is raised to 90. When the heart beats, it dilates and contracts alternately. The heart is a unique muscle that comes into existence just a few days after conception. It is formed after a few days when the foetus begins to grow and surprisingly, it starts beating immediately. And from then on for 40, 70, 80 years - as long as you live – it will keep on beating non-stop. This is a non-stop train that keeps running inside. As every instrument needs power to run, the heart too needs energy to beat. The most incredible thing is that in one of its four chambers, there is an area where electricity is produced and gets distributed to the other parts. So the heart produces its own energy. This does not happen in the brain, as it is powered by the blood that circulates in it. The brain does not have any mechanism to produce its own energy. The heart is the only organ in the body that makes and distributes its own energy.

The Upanishads have repeatedly said that the seat of the soul and that of consciousness in the human body is in the heart – not in the brain. Even Sri Krishna says: 'O Arjuna, look in your heart. You will find me there.' Sri Krishna did not ask him to search in the brain. The heart is truly unique. Awareness and consciousness may reside in the brain, but the scriptures and even brahmanvetas like Ramanna Maharishi say that the jivatman resides in the heart.

Heart is the Lifeline for Existence

The brain is dependent on the blood supply from the heart for its normal functioning. The blood also reaches other parts of the body and that is how they are able to function. If the blood supply to the brain is suspended even for just three minutes, the body parts that are controlled by the diseased brain will be paralyzed.

Another fact is that the part of the brain that suffers a stroke due to oxygen depletion cannot be revived. Just three minutes of suspension in blood supply and 80% patients die on their way to the hospital. Those who survive will lose one faculty or the other - they may suffer from paralysis, blindness, loss of speech or loss of sensations. Some will become no better than vegetables - they can see, hear and breathe, but there is no possible communication with the family. When there is no contact with the self, how can there be any contact with anyone else? Now here science is not clear about what keeps them alive - are these stroke survivors living on will power and resolve, or does some divine power keeps them going?

The working of the brain is dependent on blood supply, and the entire job of pumping the blood is done by the heart. Now when the heart is depleted of oxygen, it will naturally stop its normal function, for it requires oxygen for its own needs. The heart generates and uses its own electricity very well, but when the oxygen it receives through the blood does not reach it on time, the resultant situation is called heart disease. So heart disease is the shortfall in oxygen supply to the heart. But why should there be a shortfall in oxygen? If the blood vessels are narrow or if there is a clot in the blood, then the blood flow will slow down leading to lesser oxygen availability.

During Ram Rajya, the rule of Sri Rama, a dog once complained that a brahmin had beaten him for no reason. In those days, anyone and everyone were free to air their grievances. Sri Rama asked the dog to decide the brahmin's punishment. The dog said that the brahmin should be made the head of a temple or religious institution. "Are you punishing him or rewarding him?" asked Sri Rama. The dog said, "The day he becomes the head of a temple or religious institution, his pride and ego will grow. He is not the sort to do any good deeds. When he will live off people's donations, he will not need to labour either."

What a far-sighted thinking – this was the dog of Rama Rajya – no ordinary being. He said, "When he will sit in one place and eat, he will become lazy and his body will become diseased. When he will become the head of a religious institution or temple, he will be worshipped and revered and that will lead to pride, egotism and a feeling of power. He will grow attached to his material possessions and his disciples and priests. In this way, even his mind will become diseased. As the head, he will become involved with matters of administration and will have no time for the pursuit of knowledge. Being a brahmin, if he is unable to gain knowledge or practice it, then his punishment is that all avenues to knowledge should be closed to him. He must get all the physical comforts and respectability, so that both his body and mind become diseased."

There is a profound meaning in this story. A poor man has very little money and therefore he cannot afford to eat much or eat fried, processed, packaged and oily food. Even if he gets an opportunity to eat, his physical labour keeps his blood from thickening or clotting. So if you are wealthy and have access to fried rich food, then you have to be extra cautious - so do keep a check on your lifestyle.

Are you sure that you have not been cursed like the brahmin to sit and eat and not even lift a finger? Sedentary lifestyle accompanied with wrong food choices is detrimental for health. Wealth brings pride and material possessions, and over-indulgence in these brings disease.

When there is a shortfall in the supply of oxygen to the heart, that condition is called as IHD (Ischaemic Heart Disease), the term angina is often used as a synonym. This produces symptom of a sharp pain in the chest. Now, a very interesting fact about angina pain is that it can be managed, but only by such a person who knows how to control the rate of respiration. In case of angina attack, a person who has faith in his God and Guru will never panic. If such a person feels discomfort or pain in his chest, then very calmly, without fear, he should take deep breaths. Just as in yoga nidra, he should start moving his consciousness throughout the body. Or else he should start reciting the mantra with every inhalation and exhalation. This way, an aspirant can control the angina pain successfully. But the question arises: why should someone who practices all the yogic techniques which I have just mentioned ever suffer from angina?

Get Ready to Cure Yourself

Those who have ruined their health and are now realising that this mistake can be corrected, must give great importance to the methods of rejuvenation that I am teaching here. You must also understand that, the more you breathe calmly, the more you keep your mind calm and steady; the more mantra japa you do, the healthier you will become.

The wise ones know that this human body is a grace of the Lord, a gift, and therefore one should use it respectfully. Those who say that they do not have time for all this must realise that they are preparing for their grave. If a person says that he cannot resist fried food, cannot eat on time, cannot give up eating stale food and cannot sleep on time – well, it is his wish and his life! If he wants to end it, there is nothing anyone can do. India is a democratic country where everyone has the right to live - and to die!

The chances of IHD (ischaemic heart disease) rise in cases of emotional upsurge. Emotional surge is connected with home, office, children, spouse, neighbours, and relatives - you are competing with all to prove yourself to be number one. You are attached to them and you dsire to be loved and praised by all and criticised by none; you wish to be respected by all and never wish to respect anyone. If you salute someone, that too is with a selfish motive which could be to gain the power to dominate others.

What can the poor heart do? See how you have entangled the poor heart in a thousand attachments! This can only lead to oxygen depletion or a heart attack wherein muscles of a certain area of heart do not receive oxygen at all. It's very painful and the pain spreads from the chest to the jaw or to the arms. If a person who has a heart attack is promptly taken to a hospital or receives immediate medication, it is possible to save his life.

Heart attack is essentially angina or ischaemic heart disease – this is a consequence of lack of required amount of oxygen, which damages the heart muscle and affects its pumping action. The heart forgets to beat! The pain of a heart attack is very severe and there are several medications for it. If the heartbeat stops completely, it can sometimes be revived with an electric shock – however, for all these treatments to be effective, the patient must reach the hospital in time.

Symptoms of Heart Attack

I feel everyone should be aware of the symptoms of heart attack. If you suffer from diabetes, high blood pressure, heart problems or angina, you must warn your family members, friends and associates that if they ever see such symptoms in you, they should immediately arrange to take you to a hospital - as you may be in too much pain to speak at that time. So, they should be warned of your condition. You were not alert in time to keep your heart healthy and realised your mistake too late - at least now warn you friends and family in case of an unexpected emergency situation. Often when a person has a heart attack, the family is too distraught to react – in such situations the first few minutes are particularly crucial.

It has also been seen that the person can be saved in case of a minor heart attack. If you raise the feet of the patient who has got the attack, so that the blood flow to the heart is increased, the chances of his survival improve. There is a yogic asana called vipareeta karani (inverted pose). In this asana, you raise your legs straight up at an angle of sixty degrees. It increases the flow of blood towards the heart making it healthy. This practice should be done early morning and one should be able to hold this position for ten to fifteen minutes, but initially one may begin with a short duration and slowly increase the duration of this asana.

Medical science does not use the term 'vipareeta karani', but it has understood the fact that raising the feet is immensely beneficial in saving the patient's life. Before the situation arises where someone else has to raise your feet, be aware and raise them yourself! – i.e. practice the asana every day. Vipareeta karani is a very beautiful asana, and it is capable of healing and protecting your heart.

In the context of yogasanas, I would like to say that even if there are some asanas that you are unable to do, suppose you cannot raise your legs, then you can take the support of a chair. Raise your legs with the support of a chair and hold the posture for 30 to 60 seconds, rest and then repeat. If you keep exercising regularly, following a brisk walking schedule, even for thirty minutes, it will save you from such grave health situations.

Heart disease can also be a consequence of coronary vasospasm. Now you may ask what is a spasm? A spasm is the muscle contraction of the blood vessels. The heart beats due to oxygen, which it gets from the blood. Blood gets oxygen from the breath, therefore, correct breathing is of utmost importance. This is where the role of pranayama begins.

A faculty of cardiologists in Germany conducted extensive research in association with yogis from India, and at the conclusion of their findings they decided to rename nadi shodhana pranayama as 'coronary breathing'. Patients of angina, heart attack were taught nadi shodhana pranayama and research findings revealed that their heart function improved and the possibility of future attacks came down to almost nil. If you practice yoga nidra alongside, you will become the master of your body.

Deep Breathing is Distinct from Pranayama

Many people do not realise the difference between deep breathing and pranayama - these two are very different. We do focus on the deepening of breath, but in pranayama one uses one's concentration and resolve to awaken in oneself the pranic energy that pervades the entire universe. Pranic energy, that is the cause of all - of the body and the universe - is awakened and made to assimilate into the body. So, in pranayama we establish contact with that divine energy and use nadi shodhana to keep the heart healthy. Along with this, it is also important to take care that the nadis - subtle energy channels - run in our subtle body properly. A nadi is different from a nerve - nadi implies a flow, which in Chinese is known as a meridian; acupuncture and acupressure practitioners correct the meridians by using pressure or needle prick to heal. When you correct the flow of pranic energy, you will realise that diseases occur only where the pranic energy is blocked in meridians.

Motoyama - a Japanese scientist - invented an instrument that can map the meridians and their activities. With the help of a graph, it has become easier to identify where the flow in the meridians is obstructed. The physical body we see is not all there is to the body - there is another body called the pranic body. The physical body is renewed, energised with food and oxygen, but the pranic body too needs our attention. Any disease suffered by the physical body first manifests in the pranic body. If only one could check this and know the way to treat the disease right in the pranic body, it wouldn't even manifest in the physical body.

Motoyama's research was based on the principle that if we can identify a disease in the pranic body and treat it before it develops, then the human body will never fall ill in the first place itself.

Beneficial Techniques of Reiki, Acupuncture, Acupressure

You will be surprised to know that the Chinese civilization is almost as old as the Indian. Chinese scholars who understood the working of the prana called it 'chi'. Chi practitioners were paid a monthly retainer by people to examine them on a regular basis in order to prevent disease; if a person fell ill, the practitioner had to refund the fee back to the patient. The chi practitioner's only job was to study the pranic body and treat any disease arising at that level. He would use any method of treatment he felt was appropriate: acupressure, acupuncture, reiki, energy transmission, pranic healing, etc. No medicines or drugs were used - only mind power and an understanding of the meridians were involved in the cure. If despite this anyone fell ill, the practitioner had to compensate the patient. He even had to hang a lantern outside his place of practice to inform people that he was not a top class practitioner and that people in his area had fallen ill.

The responsibility of health of the citizens was placed in the hands of chi practitioners. They were not to treat a patient only when he fell ill, but were to ensure that he did not fall ill in the first place. Try looking for such a practitioner in your area today – you will face nothing but disappointment.

In India these days, if you have the smallest health complaint, you are asked to get a hundred tests done and this is followed by prescribing a bag full of medicines – 2 pills before breakfast and 2 after breakfast; 2 pills in the afternoon, 2 in the evening and 2 at night! It is a full time job to manage the medication - once this process starts it never stops. Once you start medication for blood pressure, after some time your body becomes resistant to it. Then the drug is changed, dosage is changed – but the medication never stops.

If you remain alert, aware and live your life sensibly, you will never fall ill. Secondly, methods like reiki, acupuncture and acupressure etc. are also very beneficial to deal with any obstruction in chi flow. If you have an attitude of healing, then you must learn these methods – for yourself and for others too.

In the human body – particularly in the male body – there is a hormone called testosterone, which is the male sex hormone. Men who are aggressive, over-ambitious and want to become millionaires overnight have an increased secretion of testosterone. This has a direct effect on the brain.

The human body has receptors, which are sensitive to hormones, and they pick up the testosterone from the blood. A worldwide survey was conducted to determine the cause of increased incidences of heart attack in people in the age group of 25 to 45 years. It was found that all the people in the study group were over-ambitious, workaholics, pushy, social climbers who over-indulged in food, alcohol, smoking and late night parties. What does a person do when he is awake till late night? Either he will drink and dance or indulge in sex. In both cases, he is creating a toxic environment in his body, which has direct implications for the heart.

There is a limit to which our blood vessels and nerves can withstand testosterone - if this limit is crossed, it may cause distress to the entire heart. Staying calm and relaxed is essential for the wellbeing of the heart. Whenever you start shouting around in your house or office, you are increasing the risk of a heart attack. Those who gamble and place bets on cricket are raising the risk of a heart attack. Gamblers are a strange lot - they can even bet on kites on Basant Panchami - a festival when people fly kites!

The desire for wealth and worship of money has made you so blind that you equate wealth with success. What kind of success is this? Whenever you have to face difficult times you get agitated, lose all control and shout like a crazy dog. When you fail in your pursuits then you get depressed and shattered and every time when you go through such wide mood swings - whatever may be the reason - it is your body and health that get damaged. Try to be as cool as a cucumber, keeping your head and heart calm. Do not get agitated for any reason.

In a study conducted by Texas University, a small dose of testosterone was administered to rats over a period of time. Even the poor rats started suffering heart attacks. Poor rats and monkeys – how ill treated they are in laboratories! Animal rights activists and animal lovers never buy any cream, powder, shampoo or any product that has been tested on animals. In America and Europe, there is a very active lobby that checks upon pharmaceutical companies if they are inflicting any atrocities on animals. Many people are very conscious before buying any product - they see if it has been tested on animals. So companies have to label their products: 'not tested on animals' or 'against animal testing'. If you wish to use a product, test it on humans - why make mute animals suffer? Some people feel that human life is more precious than that of a rat or a monkey.

Most of the cosmetics are first tested on monkeys. The monkey is tied up in chains and the cosmetics are applied to its face. Then the experiment is carried out with higher percentages to determine the reaction. If there is no reaction, the concentration is further increased. Lipstick and eye shadow is applied to the poor hapless monkey, which has been tied up in chains. Monkeys are illegally exported from India to Europe, USA and various other countries for this very purpose.

Internal Beauty is Better Than External Beauty

If you are not naturally beautiful, no amount of makeup in the world will make you beautiful! Beautifying the exterior is a waste of time, money and effort. Beautify your inner being, if you must. You do not need synthetic cosmetic beauty aids; use the natural products that nature has bestowed us with.

Once a yogi from South India came to meet me and we were sitting around talking, when the subject veered to beauty products. He was extolling the benefits of using turmeric. Instead of soap, if one uses paste made of turmeric, groundnut or coconut oil then the skin will glow and no skin diseases will occur, as turmeric has anti-fungal and anti-septic properties. Commercially made soaps have high amount of chemicals, which dry up the skin and in due course of time, you will need to apply more moisturizers for dry skin, which will again be laced with chemicals.

A sage friend once told me that he has never used any oil or soap on his body and with mere pranayama practice his body secretes enough oil – thus keeping his skin supple and moist.

Some people have bad body odour, which cannot be masked by perfumes, deodorants or perfumed soaps. Have you ever wondered what could be the cause of body odour? It is the toxins in the body and faeces, which is stuck in the large intestine. If you are in good health and not suffering from any disease, then maybe you can try the following detoxification diet regiment: stay on a diet of lemon and carrot juice for three days - on the third day the large intestines will get cleared. You may wonder how the bowel will be cleared when you have not eaten anything. It is the accumulated faeces that get eliminated. In naturopathy, enemas are administered to clear the bowel. In some cases, people are carrying six to seven kg of faeces in their colon!

If there is so much of waste matter inside you, your breath is bound to smell, you can hardly expect it to be fragrant! Man indulges in strange and unintelligent behaviour; he seems to be helpless. He tries to camouflage body odour with a perfume, or a bath – neither will be of any use. Correct your diet and do varisara dhauti (shankha prakshalana) - you will notice the change in 4 or 5 days as you will become free of bad odour. If your diet is healthy, sleeping habits are good and bowel movements are regular, it is even possible that your body begins to emanate a gentle natural perfume.

Mahavira's body emanated a natural fragrance. It is said that even Buddha's dead body had a natural fragrance. Now why their bodies were fragrant whereas your smells foul? This is so because if the body and mind are pure, unpleasant smells are not possible.

Buddha lived the life of a bhikshu - monk; he ate once a day and that too before sunset. Moreover, even for that one meal, he had to walk miles. He would walk miles to collect and eat the bhiksha - and then he would walk all the way back to his 'vihar' - dwelling. Could he ever put on weight? How could he ever suffer from diabetes? Can you imagine him getting angina? It is just not possible! His body and mind were balanced; therefore there was little possibility of disease. It is not that he could never fall ill – after all, Ramanna Maharishi did suffer from cancer. The message I am trying to convey is that following a healthy lifestyle to include yogasanas, pranayama markedly reduces the chances of diseases happening.

Raja yoga says that if you perform the cleansing techniques, then the chances of your falling ill are reduced even further. A disease like cancer to is not imported into the body; it is created in the body itself. If you are relaxed and you regularly practice yogasanas and meditation, then the chances of getting cancer are negligible.

The most important practice, to protect you from these heart diseases, is yoga nidra. Memories and impressions of several incarnations lie in your subconscious - making your mind restless, unhappy and bewildered. In spite of having everything, there is a feeling of emptiness. It is a different matter that soon this confusion, this madness starts appearing normal to you!

Let me give you an example: Some guest came to visit a person who lived near the railway tracks. At night, when a train passed by, the ground shook, the windows and doors rattled and the guest started screaming that there was an earthquake. The host said, "Just relax. This is no earthquake, just a train passing by!" The poor guest was unable to sleep all night, as every 2 to 3 hours a train would pass by. After spending a troubled night, the next morning, the guest asked his host, "How do you manage to sleep? I was up all night. If you had provided me with a drum and cymbals, I could have done 'mata ka jagaran' – the night vigil!"

The host replied, "Well, to tell you the truth, if we ever go to a place where there is no sound of a train, we cannot sleep at night. So we carry a recording of train sounds with us; we have a system that plays a train sound every one hour - that is how we are able to sleep when we visit other places!"

For such people, the sound of passing train is not noise, it is normal! Similarly, some people take their chaotic mind to be normal. A gentleman once told me that his blood pressure is 180/120 and that is normal! If this is normal, then what is abnormal?! He said that at first he was comfortable with blood pressure of 140, but then it started rising, so he took medication. At that time his blood pressure was 160 - people wondered how he could stand and walk! There is no limit to human delusion!

If you consider your abnormal condition to be normal, I salute you! I feel most people do not know what normal is - that is why so many people are ailing today. They say nothing will happen to them because they are brave and their parents and grandparents lived to be eighty. How many conjectures!

You must understand very clearly that if you wish to remain healthy, you must adopt the wonderful measures prescribed by yoga as being necessary for life. If you do not do so, you are creating extremely difficult circumstances for yourself.

We were talking about nadi shodhana pranayama. Have you ever wondered why our nose has two nostrils and not one? This is because the right and left nostrils perform different functions; they activate the sympathetic and parasympathetic nervous systems.

Experiments have revealed that if you close the right nostril and breathe through the left, then the right hemisphere of the brain is activated. An American cardiologist named David conducted the following experiment: An EEG was connected to the subject's head and he was made to do nadi shodhana pranayama; a graph was recorded at the other end. It was found that when the subject breathed through the left nostril, the right brain was activated and when he breathed through the right nostril, the left-brain was activated. As per swara yoga, the left side of the brain is activated for physical activity by activating pingala i.e. right nostril breathing and the left swara is activated for doing thinking, contemplation, fine arts and peaceful activities.

Practice of Nadi Shodhana Pranayama

First you need to sit straight, so that the movement of the diaphragm is unrestricted. When you breathe in, the diaphragm moves downwards; if you are not sitting straight, its movement will be hindered. Yogis have always recommended that one should sit with an erect spine. There is a scientific reason for this, and that is that the diaphragm should move without restriction.

The breath should be deep, slow and silent. The deeper the breath, the more the heart muscles are relaxed. For every one breath, our heart beats four times; there is a strong connection between the two. As you take deeper breaths, your heart will relax more and more. This is the natural rate of respiration, which has been disturbed by tension and mental stress. Nadi shodhana pranayama can help restore it to its natural state.

First breathe in through the left nostril, as this will help you to become calm and relaxed - always start with the left nostril and not the right one. Then breathe in through the right nostril and breathe out through the left.

The exhaled breath should be twice as long as the inhaled breath. When we breathe in, the inhaled oxygen reaches the lungs and when we breathe out, carbon dioxide is exhaled. This exchange requires some time, and you will be able to give it the requisite time if you inhale and exhale gently and slowly – taking deep and long breaths. Breathe in from the left and breathe out from the right nostril; breathe in from the right and breathe out from the left nostril – this constitutes one cycle.

Yoga is not for realising an unseen God; it is for physical and mental wellbeing i.e. to gain understanding of the body, senses and mind. As one explores deeper, yoga offers profound insight into the subconscious and inspires higher levels of attentiveness and awareness.

Paramatma has placed the sacred flame of prana in your body. Thus, human body is the real temple and this sacred flame is present in everybody. You must see this presence in everyone, everywhere and nothing else. You can see the sacred flame in others only if you first see it in yourself - so start with yourself.

When you lie down at night, relax your body with as many yoga nidra steps as you can remember, and you will soon fall asleep while doing this relaxation technique. This sleep will be a deep sleep. Deep sleep is essential, because if the sleep is light then one dreams more and the heart has to endure the excitement of the dreams. This is the reason why so many people suffer a heart attack in their sleep.

Dreams increase the possibility of a heart attack at night. During the day you exercise restraint and control over your mind, but at night this self-restraint isn't going to work and the mind takes over; it creates the visions it desires and that becomes your reality. At that time, there is a flood of sensations and the heart rate increases even in sleep. If a person has narrow blood vessels, high blood cholesterol, then the possibility of a clot occurring is more. Thus, it is even more important to relax and rest the body totally at night. If possible, try to fall asleep reciting the OM mantra. Then there is a chance that even if you dream, you will dream of your Guru, your 'ishta deva', a pilgrimage, or of meditation.

In the dream stage, the mind becomes a million times more powerful - that is why it is important to empty the mind before going to sleep. Never go to bed carrying any anger, argument or tension - for a person may die in his sleep carrying negative emotions! Shri Krishna says in the Gita, that the state of the mind at the time of death determines the next incarnation. Therefore, you must meditate before you go to sleep; at bedtime, you must do nadi shodhana. It will help calm your brain and give you a deep sleep.

There is a query from a lady who says that she falls asleep while doing yoga nidra. She wants to know what to do in order not to fall asleep.

For this you need to train yourself to be alert, and that comes with practice. Yoga nidra relaxes the body greatly and as you are already lying down, so to feel sleepy is no calamity. Do not worry - perhaps your body requires such deep sleep and that is why you fall asleep.

As your consciousness starts getting rid of all baggage and tensions, as the level of your awareness increases, the level of your alertness too will start increasing. Then, there will be no question of falling asleep in yoga nidra. If you fall asleep now, there is nothing wrong with that either; if you feel sleepy then go to sleep. Others may be disturbed if you snore, but if you are going to worry about what others have to say about you – good or bad - then you are still living in your own deluded world, and have not entered the world created by your Guru.

In the Guru's world, such things carry no importance. Whatever happens in the course of your meditation is only your concern - others have nothing to do with it. There is no dearth of ignorant people - they are all around you – who will ridicule you. There is no sense in getting angry with them, you can only pity them.

At the time of doing yoga nidra, make a firm resolve that you will not fall asleep - keep reminding yourself of it. My voice will be your greatest support, but the trouble arises when I am silent and you have to count your breaths - as soon as I leave you to your own resources, you fall asleep. It is just a sign of the fact that you are not yet fully alert and aware – sleep in yoga nidra is just your report card that you lack power of resolve. If your body has been deprived of sleep for a long time, then initially in yoga nidra this paucity of sleep will be covered up. Once that has been resolved, then it is possible that you will not sleep.

Words of wisdom alone do not lead you to God. So if you feel sleepy, I will not condemn it – maybe you need sleep. Next time when you do doze off, remember to make your resolve firmer. Sleep does not hinder yoga nidra – however, if you fall asleep, you do miss the subtle stage between waking and sleep, which you are supposed to keep a track of. But as your practice progresses every day, the degree of your awakening will also rise.

The mind becomes anxious about every little thing. You are tense if you cannot sleep and tense if you fall asleep while doing yoga nidra! Forget all your tensions – put them aside and gently enter the realm of yoga nidra. This will strengthen your heart and will give you optimum health benefits.

CHAPTER 6

Your Questions Answered

Seeker: For the past 5 years, I have been getting my Lipid Profile checked regularly. My HDL, LDL, thyroid and sugar levels are normal. I have a desk job. I jog for 20 minutes in the morning; do suryanamaskara, kapalabhati pranayama and yoga nidra to keep myself fit. I do not eat too many sweets or oily food. Despite this my triglyceride levels are high.

Gurumaa: When the liver does not function normally, the lipid metabolism gets deranged. Your lipid profile is not just related to what you eat, but how well your liver metabolises the food is also of great significance. Hence, it seems strange that despite what you have said about jogging for 20 minutes, doing kapalabhati pranayama, suryanamaskara and eating low fat food, your triglycerides are raised.

When the liver does not function optimally, the normal lipid metabolism is disturbed and hence despite eating low fat food, the serum cholesterol and triglyceride levels rise. This means that you have to first ensure that your liver is functioning optimally. If the liver continues to malfunction, the 'bad' cholesterol (LDL) levels will keep rising and before long the arteries will get clogged up and constricted. This will be hazardous for your health in the future. The liver is the third most important organ in our body. I will not go into the details of how the liver functions, but will advise that if you treat your liver, the lipid levels will automatically come to normal.

Allopathic doctors generally prescribe liver tonic as this is one of the most preferred medications known to them for any diagnosed liver disease.

Ayurveda can help in such cases with medicines like arogyavardhini, punarnava mandur - these are very good ayurvedic medicines. But do consult an ayurvedic practitioner to determine the dosage and other relevant medicines too that might be required.

In cases of liver diseases, you may consult a good ayurvedic doctor and take the medicines as per his/her advice. Generally within 15 to 20 days, one will get relief in the hands of an experienced ayurvedic consultant. However, nowadays, it is difficult to find an accomplished ayurvedic consultant. Moreover, the current practitioners are more interested in making money unlike those that used to be in China who would refund the fees back to the patients if their disease could not be cured. Today, doctors want money, whether or not the patient is cured. Medicine is a noble profession and a doctor should be a healer, one whose heart is filled with empathy and compassion, one who cannot see the patient in pain and tries his level best to alleviate the suffering. I don't want to criticise anyone, but nevertheless these days for monetary gain, a majority of the doctors would rather have patients coming to them again and again. I would like every doctor to be humane and kind. In the absence of these two virtues, a doctor is not worthy of being called a doctor.

The drug companies are only interested in getting their branded drugs sold. They not only give the doctors samples of drugs, but shower them with expensive gifts, club memberships etc., which is in a way, bribery. Every company wants to push sales and it is the doctor who prescribes, so he has to be kept happy.

Moreover, some drug companies actually target chemists rather than doctors and bribe them to preferentially sell their brands to the gullible patients. The chemists therefore start advising the patients that the medicine prescribed by the doctor is not available any more and is now sold under a new name – it is the same drug, but with a different name. One drug is cheap, the other expensive; so either the doctor or the chemist is being appeased by companies. One way or the other, pharma companies have to sell their drugs; to do so they use whatever means that are at their disposal. This is a kind of business collaboration between the drug companies, doctors and pharmacists.

I reiterate that I don't want to criticise chemists or doctors - they too have to earn a living and support a family. However, I do want people to be aware of these issues and maintain good health; one should be able to deal with disease intelligently, using home remedies. There are simple home remedies that a wise housewife should be aware of and know the health benefits and medicinal value of all the vegetables, fruits and spices that she uses daily.

The way food has been cooked at home affects the health of the entire family. For example, repeated frying in the same pool of cooking oil and the ingestion of this burnt oil which is toxic will but naturally lead to ill health.

In yoga there is an asana called ardhamatsyendra asana, which has a direct affect on the liver. The other asanas that are beneficial for the liver are: bhujangasana, sarpasana, mandukasana, shashankasana and makarasana. Nadi shodhana pranayama is very important too, and should be practiced every day and the benefits of doing this regularly surpasses the benefits of doing other pranayamas.

During winters you wear warm clothes – sweaters, shawls, etc. When winter is over you pack them away carefully. Similarly, it is important to know which pranayama should be practiced and who should not do it; when to do pranayama and when not to. If you ape the pranayama lessons you see on television, it is possible that your health may deteriorate. For example, patients with glaucoma, high blood pressure, and lower back pain should not do kapalabhati pranayama. Similarly, people suffering from lack of sleep should not practice kapalabhati at night before sleeping, as this will lead to insomnia. Remember that when your sleep is disturbed, your health starts to deteriorate. Therefore, one needs to regularly practice nadi shodhana pranayama and yoga nidra for sound sleep.

I have already talked about the pranic body. If your pranic energy is low, you cannot be healthy. Acupressure and acupuncture act on the pranic body by working on the physical body. Low levels of pranic energy means there is blockage somewhere in the flow of energy in the meridians (also called as subtle channels, not nerves), which causes diseases.

Considering the importance of these techniques, maybe in future, we will able to make a provision for these facilities here in the ashram itself. Then you will not have to run around searching for them. There is a tradition in the reiki practice, that when you learn it or teach it, there should be no exchange of money. Can you name a single reiki teacher or practitioner who does not charge money? Reiki is big business today! So before paying money to learn reiki, it is crucial to know if you have the healing power within you. You can do charity only if you have money in your pocket. Similarly, you can heal others only if you have compassion and energy within you.

On the lighter note, I narrate this story: A gentleman, who is a photographer, had come to the ashram requesting a photo session. He said, "Gurumaa, please make a blessing stance." I asked why and he replied that it looks very good and pleases people. He named a few gurus whom he had photographed, and said they had all given this pose and it always sells more. People want reassurance, and the photograph in blessing pose reassures people that the guru is always there for them! Just imagine the guru's photograph in a blessing pose hanging in your house. You come home distraught and see the guru blessing you. Well, this is definitely going to soothe your tense nerves that now everything is going to be all right!

Once a sardarji, who was a transporter told me this story. He wanted to sell his truck and was asking for seven lakh rupees for it. The buyer was offering only four lakhs saying that the truck was old, and even the engine had been overhauled. Just then the seller spotted Guru Nanak's photograph which was hung in his office and he said, "Neither seven nor four, let us settle for five lakhs and see even Guru Nanak is sealing it with his hands – five fingers." The buyer was also a Sikh and then Guru Nanak's photograph! Hence, both agreed!

Perhaps the buyer did not have that much money; perhaps the seller did not want to sell for less, but once they involved the guru, they both agreed. Later the sardarji admitted that his truck was worth only four lakhs. Now just see, he does a fraudulent deal and includes the guru in it! I have many tales to tell about this so-called 'blessing pose', but I do not play games. I declined to give any such pose for a photograph that could be misused so easily. Although it is true that if a person wants to, he will misuse anything any way and anyhow.

As we are talking about photographs, I will narrate another incident: a gentleman told me that there was an excise raid on his office in his absence. He said, "When I arrived, I was very worried to see what was happening in my office; I almost fainted. Then the excise officer supported me and said that I should not worry. He suggested that we should sit down and talk. When we went into my office and sat down, the officer saw your photograph behind my desk and said, 'Oh! Gurumaa! Do you know her?' I said, "Yes, she is my guru." The officer said, "I listen to her often and would really like to meet her." I said I had just returned from the ashram the previous night. As it happened, someone from the ashram called me at that very moment and I said 'Jai Gurudev'. As soon as I put the phone down, the officer said, 'Look, now that we have come here, we will not return empty-handed. But you are a great devotee so I have just one request that next time you go to the ashram take me along.'" The gentleman then said that, "Those people could not take the bribe they intended to, and I was saved from a great problem – my license could have been cancelled." A simple photograph of mine turned out to be so valuable! How people exploit such things for their own gain!

The excise officers had come to collect a bribe but were dissuaded on seeing my photograph; the gentleman in question made no effort on his part to do so. It is pure coincidence that they sat in the room with my photograph and that the phone call from the ashram came at that precise moment.

The photographer asked why I was refusing when so many gurus had complied. I said, "They are not gurus, they are maha gurus; why do you compare me with them? I am nothing!"

It is strange to be photographed in the blessing pose because this mudra – this pose – means concentrating your energy in the palm of your hand and then transmitting it. It is similar to adjusting antenna of your mobile phone or car in order to improve the reception quality.

Do you remember the days when the TV antenna was fixed on the roofs of houses? A strong breeze and the antenna would shift and there went your picture and one had to go up and down adjusting the antenna!

Suppose you keep adjusting the antenna without connecting it to the TV? How do you expect to get a picture? This actually happened: A family kept turning the antenna right and left for a long time, but could not get a picture. Then a child called out: "Mummy, the wire is disconnected from TV." Similarly, how can someone who does not have energy transmit it to another?

A guru may have the energy to disperse, but if a person is unable to receive it, or lacks the faculty to receive – his receiving capacity is not developed – then how can the guru help him? This means, that when the guru is ready to transmit the energy and the receiver is capable of receiving it, then this exchange is possible. This transmission of energy through the hand can help cure physical ailments as well. This is also the principle of reiki and pranic healing and this should not involve exchange of money.

The healer enjoys this energy and passes it on to the patient - both dwell in one energy zone, both enjoy a great moment. How can the healer charge for something like this? But some people have an opinion that if they don't charge, people will not give this therapy the due importance, again it is a lame excuse.

In my opinion, every true reiki master is a sage. But he is a sage only if he is wise, knowledgeable, devoid of ego, and he is neither attached to the world nor interested in making money.

Fear Alone Breeds Sorrow

The concept behind this workshop is to see how you can use the knowledge gained here to help the body that has become diseased due to an undisciplined lifestyle. If you live in fear of another heart attack, your fear will not allow you to reach this far; you will never leave home alone.

I find it strange that after listening to such profound wisdom and knowledge, a person can still live an undisciplined, unhealthy life. And that too in fear!

Defining a sage, Shri Guru Tegh Bahadur says:

He fears none and frightens none.

And here you are fearful for your own heart and cholesterol! Life can never flourish or be fulfilling if lived in fear. You will never be happy in such a situation, for happiness springs from within; it is not dependent upon external factors. Life would be simpler if one could derive real happiness from within and not by possessing material objects. If you believe that wealth or hoarding things will bring you happiness, then there is no one more deluded than you.

Performing Worldly Duties and Activities

Sometimes situations arise in which our societal life is dependant on others. You are bound to have some interaction with the people around you – there is no getting away from that. You may keep away from your friends, but how will you avoid your office colleagues with whom you interact daily; with whom you have business associations and spend around seven to eight hours every day? Whether they are nice or not nice, their attitude - positive or negative – it is sure to affect you accordingly. So, if you start receiving positivity and negativity from your colleagues, what will happen to you? You will burden yourself with all that you receive.

If someone praises you, you happily accept the compliment. The truth of the matter is that you never grew up and perhaps never will.

Have you seen a young child recite a poem: 'Twinkle twinkle little star…..' the parents are thrilled! They praise the child who feels great because of this appraisal and he asks if he should repeat it. So he recites it again, and every one claps and the child feels very happy. After ten minutes he wants to recite it again, but now everybody says: 'enough!' The child is confused; a short while ago they were all praising him, so what happened now?

You may have noticed that it is difficult to coax children to do something, but once they get going, it is more difficult to stop them. The child's brain is unable to comprehend why he is being asked to stop. The child within us never grows up – it remains forever a child. You may have grown up physically, but the child inside you still seeks approval and appreciation.

Wife is delighted when her husband praises her cooking skills. So, learn this art - eat burnt dal and stale roti, but exclaim 'wonderful!' Just this much is enough to get her to adore you! Of course she is aware of the quality of her cooking! But the praise you shower on her is like concretising the foundation of your marriage. Sometimes women too indulge in false praise of their husbands. When a husband is insulted in front of the wife, she is quick to retort: "better focus on your own!"

You build a house and expect people to come and praise it. 'How beautiful, what colours, what a design, the temple in your house is wonderful....' and the child in you is gratified. However, if someone says that it is nice but points out a flaw, you are immediately miffed. "He should take a look at his own house instead of finding fault in others." Who does he think he is - some great architect?"

To hear and speak false praises – this is a norm of the society. Keep praising each other to the skies, keep massaging each other's ego – it keeps everyone happy. The truth is not tolerated here; in fact no one dare speak the truth here. Try telling an obese woman that she is fat; "hmm, she is well-to-do!" will be the retort. If a man is of low intelligence, no one will say that he is stupid; they will say he is very simple. Why can't you come out and say clearly that he is a fool? Because that will lead to conflict and why should anyone unnecessarily buy trouble. So a fool becomes a simpleton and an obese person is well-to-do! This is how we disguise our shortcomings and turn a blind eye to them.

If you have to attend a funeral or cremation, your reaction is: "In this heat? At 4 O' clock? Well, what to do, I suppose I will have to go. If I do not then tomorrow no one will attend our funerals..."

You receive a wedding invitation. Your reaction is: "for a five-rupee card I will have to give a five hundred-rupee gift. What an expensive dinner!" Then you remember that they had given you Rs.1000. So now the problem is compounded. "How can I refuse?" Often people do not attend weddings because the money saved by not going is substantial. Sometimes they do go but keep resenting it. Such are your shallow fake social relationships!

I have seen people criticising a person, but if the same person arrives at their house, they feed him samosa! "Please eat brother, you have not eaten anything." And after he leaves you again begin to ranter: "How much he eats! I offered him once and he kept on eating it all."

Hypocrisy in Relationships

You talk ill of a person, yet you think of him, meet him – this is hypocrisy; this is a falsehood and one day will lead you into trouble. One such gentleman has written: "When my office colleagues talk against me I get so perturbed that I find it difficult to breathe. I feel like breaking someone's head. But instead, I am forced to say, 'Yes Sir'. If my boss says that I am an ass, even then I have to say: 'Yes Sir'. Why is the boss being so mean? Why is he talking so rough? Someone must definitely have upset him."

If someone scolded you harshly in childhood, you become vindictive for that person all your life. A child comes home and shows his report card; he has fared badly in several subjects. The father first gives him two slaps and then picks up the card. After reading the report, he gives the poor child four more slaps. Right through school and college the child takes a beating – he then gets a job. Then at office there is someone who is going to make his life a hell. Can such a person ever be happy deep down in his heart?

There are many women who are too busy with their own lives to give loving attention and care to the child who is left to the recourse of servants. They hand over money to the child expecting him/her to eat out in the market or in the school canteen. Such children do not receive the love, affection and compassion of their mother. A child who has never been lovingly fed by the mother, who has never been lovingly caressed and blessed by the mother, will grow up to secretly hate women and treat them shabbily.

You may have witnessed a scene like this: A woman is travelling in a rickshaw and a young chap going by a scooter or cycle slaps her back or pinches her, or passes an obscene comment. Why does he do this? Perhaps his mother never hugged him; she never patted him to sleep with lullabies; she never praised his every little achievement. When a child does not receive all this, it is little wonder that he grows up to be a criminal, a rapist and a tormentor of women. Before punishing such an individual, it is very important to psychoanalyse him. Only then we will know what all he has suffered.

Such a person cannot be in a good mental health. I have seen many tribal areas in Orissa like Puri where the women do not wear any upper garment – it reflects their poverty and partly their culture. Bare chest they go about doing their daily activities including working in open fields. No one teases them; no man even looks at them lecherously. A man who has seen his mother in this way since childhood will never give obscene look to any woman's breasts. What attraction will this child have for any other woman's breasts?

In India, mothers breast-feed their child for a long duration and the first introduction of the child towards his mother is through the mother's breasts. He receives milk from mother's breast, his hunger is satiated, and it is not only physical hunger but also emotional bonding which happens through breast-feeding. When a mother holds her child close to her and feeds the baby, the child can hear her heartbeat and feels loved. For those children who grow up in such a loving atmosphere, the bonding at the level of mind and emotions assumes greater significance compared to that at the merely physical level.

Understand the True Purpose of Life

Those people, who think that wealth and fancy homes will give happiness, are ignorant of the fact that the rat race they are running can only end in heart or liver failure. I ask you a direct question: What is your goal, your aim in life? What is important to you? Write it down on a piece of paper; what is important to you and what is the meaning of life for you?

Even if you succeed in impressing society with your money, cars, houses and offices, it will not rid you of mental stress. And your mind will always suffer from lack of love and affection because when you are so busy dealing with money matters, family life suffers. People are bereft of love, they just have sex but know this – sex is not love. Sex cannot compensate for lack of love. You might be very active sexually, but still, you remain devoid of love.

It is possible that you read many books but are ignorant of true knowledge; you listen to spiritual discourses, but are bereft of wisdom. It is prudent to remember that we cannot cheat life. Life is incomplete without essence and substance. Your mind desires bliss and relaxation. But you encourage and provoke it to join the rat race. The mind is still a child – first it found pleasure in reciting nursery rhymes, now it seeks gratification elsewhere in food, sex, wealth, power, status, etc.

I would like to tell you a story from the life of Diogenes – a staunch Greek philosopher. Alexander had sent several messages to Diogenes inviting him to meet him, but Diogenes ignored them. Finally it was decided that Alexander would pay him a visit in person. Alexander did go but he was rather miffed, so without dismounting from his horse, he said to Diogenes: "Do you not know who I am? How did you dare to refuse my invitation?"

Diogenes kept lying on the bank of the river with his eyes closed. This outraged Alexander even more as others would have immediately stood up on seeing Alexander, but this man kept lying down. Diogenes never wore any clothes and this exasperated Alexander to see that he had not even bothered to dress, in spite of being informed of the visit. Alexander's ego was bruised!

Without getting up and with his eyes closed, Diogenes said: "Yes I know who you are. You are just a drop". The body comes into existence from a drop – a single drop of the father's semen. "I know very well who you are, but I am sorry to see that you do not know who you are," said Diogenes.

Alexander did not understand what Diogenes was saying as he was only used to hearing 'Alexander the great'. However, here someone was showing him the mirror, making him face the reality he neither wanted to know nor understand. No one had ever said to him that he was just a drop!

On hearing this harsh truth for the first time, Alexander dismounted from his horse and came and sat at Diogenes' feet. Diogenes looking at him with piercing eyes said, "You are a drop now and later you will be a fistful of dust. Just look at your reality. Now ask what you want to ask. I have already told you the truth of your being."

If you look around, at any corner of any city, you will find someone or the other saying: "You don't know who I am." Recently I was in a city in Punjab where I had gone to address a gathering. A huge crowd had collected and it became difficult to control it. Also present in large numbers were the so-called elite of the city – people of assumed importance. I was sitting patiently waiting for everyone to come and settle down. It would be amusing to see the variety of gathered egotists! Just as models show-off their clothes in a fashion parade, here was a parade of narcissism! I was ready to watch it all. When they started coming in, it was like a competition, on who was more pompous and conceited than the other. When it was time for me to address the gathering, I said I would not meet any more people and asked for the door to be closed. Just then a man walked up to the gate and told the person at the gate that he was a special associate of the S.S.P. With great style he kept twirling his moustache and saying: "You don't know who I am." The attendant said, "OK, but you wait here, you can't meet her now. When she passes by you can see her, but you can't meet her."

I have never seen a creature like him before. People send their visiting cards or they send a message, but no one talks with such arrogance.

Who are the people you are surrounded by? Whom do you wish to impress? Who do you want to display your stature to? Whose approval do you wish to gain? Get out of this self-created trap. You are always playing the number game. In school, if you got 4 out of 10 and someone else got 6, you would say: "If I take tuition I will get 6 out of 10." So you work hard so that in the future you may score 10 out of 10. This conditioning since childhood makes you crave for recognition and approval; it makes you desire to become an object of envy. You squirm in hatred and wish ill to those who are a step better off than you. What a childish non-sense!

Lifestyle Changes are Necessary

People who are locked up in asylums are not the only ones who are mentally ill. The truth is that they have crossed the fine line between sanity and insanity while you are just outside that line– that is the only difference. This is a mad society of mad people. See how they fight: 'This one said that to me,' 'that one said this to me,' 'I'll see him,' 'I'll show him......'

If this is not stark madness, what is? The madness in your mind is making your body sick. So before rushing to a doctor, sit quietly, sort out your brain, rectify your thinking and amend your lifestyle. It is then that you will begin to feel healthy.

There is no need to worry. But do not be like the laughter club members who laugh from 8 to 10 am and still spend the rest of the day grumpy! The laughter generated by a laughter show is also fake. If you laugh at a comedian's comedy, it is bogus laughter. True laughter springs from the heart like a fountain, and this laughter will rejuvenate every cell in your body. So, whenever you are sad, angry, depressed, low or vengeful, just slap your head and say: "You fool, what are you doing?" Your thoughts can make your body ill.

Seeker: My heart is enlarged and its pumping action has reduced. I was asked to get an angiogram done. When the angiography was done, they found no blockages and the doctor said that I could be treated with medicines.

Gurumaa: Yesterday, I spoke about plaque, which is the white material deposited between your teeth. When the plaque gets into the blood stream and reaches the vessels it causes problems that we never pay attention to. The older generation still cleans their teeth with neem twigs, and you are caught up with toothpastes! 'Well, if a certain celebrity uses particular toothpaste, so must I.' Here too you are being a copycat – a tendency that is exploited by companies who provoke you into buying their products. They say: "Use this hair oil." But why? "Just because a certain film star does!"

A product sells on the endorsement of a celebrity – a cricketer or a film star. Everyone wants to buy it, because by association they feel rich and famous. Intelligent decision-making is none of consumer's concern these days - endorsement sells products.

Look at the irony that no one gets endorsements from intellectuals; society is not interested in them. Society is only concerned with external show and money, therefore, they get glamorous people for endorsements. Today, it is not the product that is getting endorsed; important thing is who is endorsing the product.

Plaque is the debris in the mouth which eventually pollutes the blood – so it is important to rinse your mouth whenever you eat something. People of the older generation rinse their mouth several times after eating. They roll the water in the mouth around twenty to twenty-five times to remove every bit of food caught between the teeth.

A well-known dentist in Delhi once told me that even today he uses his grandmother's remedies, and has never suffered from any gum disease. This remedy is to mix a bit of salt in mustard oil and to gently massage the gums with it. He still uses a neem twig instead of toothpaste. After meals he brushes his teeth, because using the neem takes time. At that time he was over 60 years, and all his teeth were fine. This is what he suggests to his patients too. But people lack time – not the time to eat, but the time to clean their teeth!

The plaque that collects in the mouth causes the blood vessels to narrow down, and mind it, this does not show up in any ECG either. Even the best doctors will be unable to see this in an angiogram. If there is no problem, then why do an angiography?

You have written that according to doctors there is no blockage, surgery is not required and the echocardiogram (often referred as ECHO) too is normal. All you need is regular medication.

As I have mentioned earlier, one of the drugs used is diuretic, which increases frequency of urination but has an adverse effect on the kidneys. So whenever you visit your doctor, ask him about the side effects of the medicines he has prescribed.

Sedentary lifestyle, eating junk food and not exercising - all these things in combination will give serious trouble. So keep a check on your diet also.

I will cite an example: During Diwali, you generally receive several packets of dry fruit, which usually are placed on the coffee table in the living room. The TV is on, and you wish to munch, the box is lying in front of you. Do you know the amount of cholesterol in one cashew nut? If asked, you will say you ate just a few, but while watching TV one loses track of how much one eats. Almonds, cashews are very high in cholesterol. And you eat them with relish! Now how can it be that you will not have coffee with it and how can you have coffee without sugar! So you end up eating food which has a high calorific value.

If you are healthy, then almonds are good for you. Dry fruits are harmful for people who are heart patients, or who have high cholesterol – they should be cautious about their diet. One person said: "I ate only cashews." How much? He said "Only half a kg. I was watching a film and did not realise when the packet was over!"

Pay attention to your diet and try to keep it as natural as possible. There are some fruits and vegetables that are beneficial for the heart. It is interesting to note that the brain is similar in appearance to a walnut.

If you remove the shell of a walnut, you will see that it is in two parts – right and left. As the surface of the brain is ribbed, so is that of the walnut. It is as if nature is trying to tell us that if you want your brain to function well, eat a few walnuts everyday. The shape of your heart resembles a pomegranate. Its juice is very beneficial for heart patients. Bottle gourd and white pumpkin are also very useful. Drinking the juice of a white pumpkin on an empty stomach early morning, after doing asana and pranayama, thins the blood and strengthens the heart.

According to me, you should do nadi shodhana pranayama for 15 minutes in the morning and evening, along with asana. Maintain a good diet. I will not ask you to stop your medication, but do follow all these methods, which will increase your body capacity. Once the body is healthy and strong, there will be no need for medication but be watchful of your diet too.

One of the legacies of the British Raj is: bed tea! Drinking bed tea is considered a status symbol! After all, poor people don't drink bed tea – they do datun (using a neem twig) and get on with daily chores to earn a livelihood. So they eat a roti or two and set off for work – they don't drink tea. If they get a cup of tea at their work place, it is welcome, but they can do without it.

One person said he does not have a bowel movement without tea. Only when he drinks a cup of hot tea does he have a movement, not otherwise. If you start your day with tea and a newspaper, just stop to think of its ill effects: you are not giving a good start to your day. I am not asking you to stop reading the newspaper or to give up drinking tea. All I am saying is don't do it early in the morning on empty stomach.

After emptying the bowels, the first thing to enter your stomach should be something which nourishes your cells and strengthens and supports them. So correct your diet and eat more natural foods. Avoid packaged food; avoid food made with white flour, like noodles etc. You are living in India, not in America that you cannot get fresh mithai! Even so, we are adopting the trend of packaged mithai. Who knows how long ago the mithai was made, then treated with preservatives and packaged? These harmful chemicals destroy your health.

In some families where the both spouses work, the husband and wife both should be responsible for running the kitchen. If you must eat mithai, make it yourself or at least buy fresh one. Have you ever seen the place where the mithai is made? I used to go for satsang to a temple. There was a mithai shop there that was famous for its samosas. While passing by, the halwai would greet me in a loud voice. He would be sitting there in his mere dirty underwear, with hands so black it seemed they had never been introduced to soap. If not soap, he could have scrubbed them with ash, well with anything.....! With dirty hands, long dirty nails, when he rolled out the samosas, he would place the dough on his thigh, roll it, stuff it and then fry it. And people loved these samosas!

One day a lady brought samosas for me. She said, "Please eat, you must be hungry." She knew that I had come straight from college. "Sardarji's samosas are delicious, please have them." I refused politely, but she kept on insisting that I should at least try them. They maybe tasty, but how could I eat after what I had seen? They were made under such unhygienic conditions, and on top of that who knows what sentiments went into the making? Food is affected by the sentiment with which it is cooked. Your energy, whether positive or negative, affects the food you cook.

Our rishis say that one should not eat food cooked by just anyone. This is not a question of discrimination or untouchability, but because the thoughts and sentiments of the person pervade the food. Let alone chemicals; our rishis were even concerned about emotions and sentiments.

Long ago a saint was visiting our home. He asked for a glass of water, so I went and fetched it for him, but he refused to drink it. I asked why; the water was clean. He said the water was fine, but the manner in which I presented it was not acceptable to him. I asked him what to do. He said, "Go while reciting a mantra. Wash the glass, dry it and then fill it with water; keep on doing chanting even when you are climbing the stairs. If you can do this, then I will accept the water." I was just a kid at that time, so I was quite interested in doing sewa. He said, "If you want to do some service, by all means go ahead, but whatever you do – cutting the vegetables, cooking the food or making the rotis – keep chanting the mantra and one should not talk while doing this."

You may have noticed that when women are doing some work, they talk so much! They discuss the family fights and arguments – all this becomes a part of the food that is being cooked. That is why our rishis have said that one should make an offering to God before cooking and before eating. If someone cooks and eats while remembering God; if one is constantly doing naam japa, can his mind ever be ill? And the food cooked in such a way will be hallowed blessed food.

Seeker: I have had two heart attacks. Four arteries were blocked for which I had bypass surgery. There was tension in the family. Can I suffer blockages a third time? I am on medication for the last 7 years. I do not suffer from high cholesterol or diabetes. Can I stop my medication?

Gurumaa: Have you ever wondered why you ever had so many ailments - sometimes wrong diet and family tensions can take away one's zest for life. The day one's life is devoid of any happiness, one may not commit suicide, but starts longing for death.

Pay attention to this story: An English officer went to meet Hitler. Hitler always liked to show off his power and stature, so he said, "Would you like to witness my command?"
"Certainly," said the officer.

They were on the third floor, and Hitler ordered his guard to jump. He jumped without a moment of hesitation and fell to his death. The English officer was shocked. "Would you like to see more?" Before he could answer, Hitler commanded the second guard to jump. Without hesitation, he too jumped to his death.

Hitler said, "This is my control over the whole of Germany. I asked one to jump and then the other. If I order the whole country, they will follow me." To further demonstrate this he called the third guard. But the Englishman caught hold of him and said, "Please do not jump, life is very precious." The guard replied, "In Hitler's rule, can a person have a life worth living?' he too jumped.

What is the point of living a life that is bereft of love, happiness, peace and joy? You will be surprised to know that in Hitler's rule, any army man in Germany could enter any home and have sex with any woman – this was the license granted to them. They could shoot anyone without fear of being questioned.

Worry Bankrupts the Life

When life is sad, tense and worrisome, a person can lose the desire to live. Then the subconscious mind brings in one disease or the other. Psychological research shows that when a person is disheartened and disillusioned, the best of medicines are ineffective. An optimistic and vivacious person rarely falls ill. If he does, he recovers fast and does not panic. When you suffer from phobias, manias and depression, you become highly susceptible to allergies. Allergies are related more to your mind than to your body.

Now this lady is saying that she is on medication for the last 7 years and does not suffer from high cholesterol or diabetes. She wants to know if she can get blockages a third time, and whether she can give up her medication. You have already had two attacks. I will not ask you to stop your medication, but I will ask you to stop even thinking of a third attack. Now you should think that it would never happen! Why should it happen? Live the way you have been taught and you will see your health improving. At the time of doing nadi shodhana, suggest to yourself that every inhalation is bringing pranic energy into your body and healing you.

This evening we will teach you a technique which will give you instant relief from increased heart rate, any sudden pain, or pain in the heart. Remember, your mind is much more powerful than your body. When we harness and use the power of the mind, the body is sure to become healthy. Just drop negative words from your vocabulary. Do not even think that something negative can happen.

Tell me honestly; aren't you worried about a third attack? Isn't that the reason why you have asked? You are convinced that it will happen a third time just because it has happened twice. I have explained this earlier that the heart disease is caused because of narrowing of blood vessels, lack of adequate oxygen supply, or a fault with the pacemaker. You have written that four arteries were blocked. In such a situation, a heart attack is hardly a surprise.

Now that it has happened, consider it a warning from nature to look after yourself. Be grateful to God, Guru and nature, whose benevolence and blessings have saved you from death and brought you here, to hear and understand what you need to do.

There are many people who do not even survive the first heart attack. It carries them to the pyre; takes them to the Ganges – it is the end of the road for them. How can I convince someone who is dead? For me to explain and for you to understand, it is necessary for you to be alive. What can be better than the fact that you are alive? If you ask a corpse, it cannot even reply whether it is well or not! It has passed into another realm; its wicket has fallen, you are still on the playing field. That is why I am bowling the balls of knowledge and wisdom to you; that is why I am talking to you of yoga and pranayama, of diet and yoga nidra and of mantra japa. Practice what I am teaching. Why do you ask if you can have a third attack? Do not even think about it.

It is said that troubles do not announce their arrival. This is true, but you already know that trouble has arrived. Now that you know, use your intellect and wisdom. The one that has come will go away one day – how long will it stay? The blockages in the arteries will go - first get rid of the thought that this can never be cured. Do not even think that it will get okay in the future; think that it is okay now. It is positively Okay.

In addition you have written that there is a gap in your spine. This can be corrected by bhujangasana, sarpasana, ushtrasana and makarasana. These asanas are not difficult, we will teach them; do them early in the morning and in the evening. In fact you can easily be in the pose and do the mantra japa along with it. Keep watching your breath or listening to music and enjoy your asanas. While watching the breath, concentrate at the point where you have problem. Imagine that the breath is going in and the pranic energy is strengthening the diseased part. When you keep up the practice of imagining that every breath carries the divine energy to your body, it definitely cures you. There is nothing that cannot be cured with right medication, right asana and pranayama.

If you say that AIDS and advanced cancers cannot be cured, I will still say that it is not a problem - if this body goes you will get a new one! Why worry? If your vehicle is old or it breaks down, what do you do? You exchange it for a new one. Old clothes are replaced with new ones. When you see those people who go around offering new utensils for old clothes, you immediately make an exchange. Similarly, as long as you can look after your body and keep it healthy, you should. With disciplined lifestyle and a firm resolve, you can keep your body healthy.

One day we all have to die. Only a yogi has the resolve to separate his pranic body from his physical body and live as long as he wishes but even a yogi will drop his body, finally. When the time comes, the body systems will shut down.

You may have learnt nadi shodhana and yoga nidra, but this game called life will be over one day – that is for sure. I am not teaching you a formula for immortality; the body can never be immortal because its very nature is transient. We are not trying to defy death. Our aim is to learn the art of living a healthy, happy, cultured and disciplined life.

I am not giving you an assurance that you will never have a heart attack. Death requires an excuse, a reason. Either the heart stops beating or the brain stops working. Do not try to defy death – it is a certainty! But as long as you are alive, you should be healthy in body and mind and when the time of death comes, accept death gracefully.

The difficulty with heart patients is that they suffer more from mental tension than from heart problems. A heart patient worries day and night about what will happen to his wife and children if he dies, or he will worry about his business affairs. Several such thoughts arise in the mind, which make you sad and dejected. Remember - the more you nurture sadness, the more stress you place on the hypothalamus – which will affect functioning of the brain. As you think, so shall your body be. Instead, you should always think positive and be optimistic- think that you are full of vitality and good health.

One of my female disciples lives in Delhi. She had a heart attack about 12 years ago. After she met me, she started doing meditation and was regular in satsang; plus being in my proximity her health started to improve. Now the situation is such that if she has the slightest problem, her doctor asks if it has been a long time since she met me! "Are you not listening to Gurumaa these days? Are you not doing your meditation?" Her doctor suggests these remedies before prescribing a medicine!

When your mind is disturbed, your health will be disturbed. Even if the body gets a disease, do not allow the mind to become sick. Some people have narrow blood vessels or a hole in the heart from birth; sometimes even 10–12 year old children have to undergo heart surgery. This is due to no fault of theirs, but if the condition exists one must go for the right treatment i.e. if surgery is required, get the surgery done. If it can be cured with medication then do not delay and pay attention to it. But do not let your mind fall sick, keep your mind healthy. If you follow my instructions, even your blocked arteries can open up gradually. But it will take time - it is not a matter that will be sorted out overnight.

Do not dwell under the misconception that you can start nadi shodhana and give up your medication simultaneously. This is absolutely wrong. For the moment you just practice the meditations taught to you, correct your lifestyle and dietary habits. After incorporating all this in your lifestyle, when you go for your routine check-up and the doctor says that everything is fine, don't be surprised! What I am trying to say is that when a doctor hands you a list of medicines, you get anxious and distraught. If words of a doctor can have that effect on you then well, I too am a doctor - of wisdom and good sense! Therefore I ask you to be sensible and judicious.

If you have mistreated and abused your body, it will get sick. If you are responsible for its deterioration, then it is certainly you who is also responsible for improving your own health.

Have you ever seen any sportsperson playing a game? A player gets hurt in a game and keeps bleeding but insists he is all right - because he wants to continue playing. Such is the fervour! Not caring about the injury he continues to play and even wins the match and jumps with joy! Next day you read in the papers that he was injured, hence will not play the next match. People are surprised because they saw him play the previous day. This is due to the fact that while playing the game there was so much enthusiasm and energy in the mind, that the pain from the injury was not perceived at all.

If a sportsman's passion and enthusiasm for the game can make him rise above the pain in his body, can you not keep yourself in a state of divine love and divine bliss? Learn to ignore trivial aches and pains in the body.

A doctor told me that a lady came to him and asked him to perform any surgery on her. Surprised, the doctor asked her as to what she meant. The lady said, "Well, what should I do? Every time I go to the club I meet ladies who have high blood pressure, heart disease, gall bladder surgery. I am the only one who has had no surgery!" The doctor refused downright saying he would do no such a thing. "If you won't do the surgery, at least call my husband in and tell him that I am not well and he should take care of me." "Why would I do that?" asked the doctor. "He doesn't come home on time, doesn't take me out, and doesn't spend time with me. If you tell him he will listen to you. I will double your fees! Just do this for me."

The doctor told me that he called her husband. So far she was fine, but when her husband entered the room, she started groaning as if she is in a lot of pain. I advice husbands to understand that if their wife is groaning, there maybe nothing wrong with their body, maybe she is seeking some sympathetic attention or an outing from the husband - long live such female characters! The more you think you are ill, the more ill you will be. On the other hand, the more you think that you have no disease, the healthier you will be. Recognise this divine power within you. Your thinking should not be pessimistic. Know this that the body is mortal and 'I' am not the body – 'I' am Shivaswaroopa.

CHAPTER 7

Listen to the Sound of Divinity Within...

The body has five sense organs (gyana indriyan) - mind is the master of senses and prana is the master of mind. Normally our sense organs are outwardly oriented and we have to turn them inwards. Hence, when you sit to do pranayama or dhyana, then choose a silent spot so that ears can be shut off from all sounds, still the body, close the eyes, and still the tongue - refrain from talking or tasting. Except for the eyes, other sense organs are comparatively easier to control – the eyes always want to see the external world, irrespective of whether it is relevant or not. Thus, when you shut the eyes, half of the work is done. Besides this, the tongue also disturbs as it cannot stay long without talking or eating. The ears too want to hear what is happening in the world - it is very important for you to get all the news! Our skin too desires good clothes, perfumes, jewellery, etc. That is why our senses are most of the time obsessed with the external world. A person's nature and his involvement in the outer world are defined by the three sense organs namely, eyes, tongue and ears, and the two action organs namely, tongue and the sex organs.

Senses can either be used wisely or one can merely abuse these faculties. If you spend a whole day in an air-conditioned office, then make it a point to spend an hour or two with nature and exercise so that you sweat profusely. However, a patient with heart disease cannot do heavy physical exercise and it is anyway not recommended. He should make it a point to routinely walk or at least take a stroll every day. However, if someone has bad knees, then he can't even walk - he should then just sit in the open and soak the senses in sights and sounds of nature - chirping and twittering of birds, breathe in fresh air or just enjoy colours of the sky and refreshing cool breeze; one should be in tune with nature.

Someday take a walk in a garden barefoot, learn to befriend the trees and talk to the flowers. You may be too old to chase butterflies but you can at least sit and watch their beautiful wings and their pretty colours. Observe the exuberant laughter of children and get so absorbed in it that you too laugh wholeheartedly. I wonder why people are so restrained. I am not talking just about you, but even here in the ashram there are people with grim and morose faces. I wonder what they have learnt till now. There is no tax on laughter, then why are people always so tense? It doesn't hurt to smile, does it? Be free from worries, and smile.

I have discussed many issues in the earlier section - what is a healthy diet, how food should be cooked, how and when to eat, how and when to sleep and why deep sleep is essential. Now I will talk about cures for diseases.

Nada Anusandhana

Nada means sound or sound waves, and anusandhana means research or experimentation. In this process, first a sound is created and then the mind is attached to it. For example, when you recite the mantra OM – you create the sound and hear it too. When you do gunjan of OM, you close the ears and hum like a bumblebee, creating the vibrations of OM sound. Once you do this, concentrate on those parts of the body where these vibrations have a special impact. If you observe carefully, you will notice that when you do gunjan after closing the ears, the deepest impact is on the throat, face and neck. As you go on observing very diligently, you will start noticing the effects of these vibrations behind the ears, on the nose, and ultimately advancing to the forehead and top of the head. Pursue the vibrations very judiciously to see from where they arise and how they disperse and pervade the different body parts. This is nada anusandhana and is also known as nada yoga. This is the first step in the practice of nada.

Of the 108 main Upanishads, the 'nada bindu' is an Upanishad wherein all the shlokas are based on nada. What is nada, how it works, what are the benefits of listening to it – all this is discussed in it.

The second stage is when you close the ears but do not create any sound; instead you endeavour to listen to the extremely subtle sound existing inside. This divine sound is constantly playing within you. However, as you are so engrossed in the external sounds, you remain unaware of this divine sound.

Once you have internalised your senses then you create a barrier of OM nada. As you go deeper in it, the mind becomes calm and tranquil. This is the time when you can focus more minutely on this subtle sound which is reverberating within you. Every sound is a current and every sound current affects our body. The sound of 'm' and 'h' benefit the vishuddha – throat chakra and anahata charkas – heart chakra; chanting of OM affects the ajña chakra; 'Ram' mantra benefits the manipuraka charka - solar plexus.

Mystic Kabir and other exalted masters have categorised this divine sound and said that in the beginning it is like the sound of the insect - cricket. Later, it is like the soft strumming of a veena, thereupon, begins to sound like the beat of a drum and finally like a conch. The beat of the drum is nothing but the sound of your own heart that becomes audible to you - 70 beats a minute!

When a doctor uses a stethoscope, he can tell whether your heart beat is normal or not, but you are unaware of your very own heart beat. It is your body, your heart - and you are unaware! Isn't it strange? One can even hear the flow of blood in the blood vessels, but for this it is essential for the mind to be silent and concentrated.

Nada yoga is an even deeper sadhana. Only those people will be able to do the nada sadhana who have first thoroughly practiced chanting of OM, followed by OM gunjan or bhramari pranayama. Alongside if yoga nidra is done, then within 6 months you may be able to do the nada yoga sadhana, provided you have done the practice with utmost sincerity. Before this it is not possible. So, please do not even try doing it, as when you will not be able to do it properly, you will get de-motivated.

OM is not a fictitious imaginative word created by the rishis - it is a sound that has not been created by anyone. It is a primordial sound that pervades every atom in the space. Bible and Gurbani bear witness to the fact that God first created the word.

In nada yoga, one attempts to catch the subtle and ethereal sounds which are present in the nature. Then there is another wonderful method to explore nada - it is called Kirtan - "to repeat".

Group Kirtan

When you sing any vedic verses or mantra, there is an upsurge of divine energy. When you sing a devotional song or a mantra with emotional fervour, it has a very therapeutic effect leading to the release of repressed emotions, while at other times it also acts as a cathartic to bring the suppressed feelings on the conscious surface of mind – one may feel like crying or vibrations may happen in the body or body may tremble, shake and sway. It can be an exhilarating experience.

Sooner or later, a shrewd therapist will create a format out of kirtan as well to heal people and then people will pay to learn 'Divine Singing Therapy'. Like reiki, kirtan too will become a business - only difference is that it will be called 'Divine Singing Therapy'. Often I feel that this is the age of packaging and not of content. We never had such packaging in markets in earlier times but today, from a child's sweets to chocolates, from clothes to phones, from scooters to cars – everything is packaged. Packaging has become the greatest marketing tool today.

Live Simple and Not Complicated

To some extent, dramatisation is good because it attracts people, but it is of utmost importance to fathom the content. To recapitulate, one can derive health benefits from kirtan and mantra chanting. Please do understand that kirtan is not done to please God, as some people would like to think - it is for enhancing your own body and mind. Kirtan is not done to please Shiva, Krishna or Rama; it normalises functioning of the endocrine and circulatory systems. While singing in love, some people begin to dance as well - if that happens, then it is indeed good for your muscles. Dancing is beneficial for everyone as it uplifts the mind, and just moving and jiving with the rhythm associated with the mantra or sanskrit verses builds up such energy that the person begins to feel ecstatic.

In your session of dance meditation here, you are not being made to dance in order to dance! Keep your attention on the rhythm and blend your own rhythm with it. If you understand words that are being sung then you will start thinking about it, and if that happens then the dance will essentially be reduced to nothing but gymnastics – like a monkey jumping around and you end up looking foolish! The music played for you at night is not randomly selected – the selection is based on some profound thinking and research.

Dance is a therapy in itself. Look at small children – despite no music, they start humming a tune and even if they don't hum anything, they may design some rhythm in their head and start jumping and swaying joyfully. Grown-ups complain the child does not sit still! You fail to understand that the natural energy of the child makes him jump, fall, run – this further strengthens his body. However, parental control begins to take away the child's freedom from day one. You scold the child for making noise: "Don't shout, don't scream." If a child will not make noise, then who will? You have suppressed your screams, you have suppressed your tears, and you have controlled your spontaneous laughter, so you tell the child not to scream, not to cry - in effect, you inhibit his spontaneity and wantonness.

A guest picked up a rasgulla and pressed it so hard with the spoon that the rasgulla went flying and landed on the floor. The child laughed out aloud. His mother slapped him hard, "Don't laugh!" Disheartened, the child went and sat in a corner. Of course the guest was embarrassed but it is only a rasgulla that has fallen! Is your self-respect so fragile that it breaks at the drop of a hat?

When the guests left, the parents started recounting the evening's events regaling each other with their comments and criticising the guest: "People don't know how to eat." Then the child spoke up: "When I laughed, you shut me up but now for the last two hours you have been laughing at the same incident. I will phone uncle and tell him that you are still laughing at him!"

You are teaching your child to be deceitful. You are telling him that it is all right to laugh behind someone's back but not to his face. Try to adopt the unfettered freedom of a child. Maturity gave you only two gifts: blood pressure and heart attack - a child does not suffer from any of these. So I suggest that once a while you must invite your friends and family for kirtan and dance – and dance to your heart's content!

Who says meditation means just sitting with your eyes shut? A religion that is devoid of fun and frolic, which does not allow you to sing and dance, is no religion - it is sheer dictatorship, exploitation. Don't live a restrained life; live freely. Don't be a slave to materialism. Don't give undue importance to material objects – they are just means to an end – they should be enjoyed but not obsessed for. After fulfilling your basic needs, if you still continue to earn, then you will only end up accumulating all those things that you do not really need and will never even use. Do a reality check and ask yourself - how many things have you bought just to show off to others!

Rulduram got married and along with the wife came a huge dowry. Ruldu was thrilled to get a new scooter, sofa and fridge. But Ruldu's mother did not unpack the things. She said she would open them at the appropriate time. Then one day she opened some of the stuff and arranged it in the house. Ruldu asked his mother for the scooter keys as he wanted to go for a ride. The mother replied, "Son, this is just for showing off to the neighbours. If you take it out, it may get spoiled and lose its glimmer. The roads are so filthy, full of mud and the tyres will get dirty. So, go walking – no scooter ride!"

Ruldu was disappointed. Then he saw the sofa in the drawing room and decided to check it out. His mother said, "Don't sit on the sofa, this is only for visitors," and she locked the drawing room. When Ruldu wanted to switch on the TV, his mother told him to use the old one, as this one would get damaged! Ruldu asked his wife to serve him dinner in the new floral decorated plates. But yet again the mother said, "It was only for visitors, "Use the old ones." Baffled Ruldu sat sulking in a corner. At night everyone went to their rooms but Ruldu kept sitting in a corner. When the mother asked him to go to his bedroom to his wife, Ruldu refused. "Why," asked his mother? "You will again say: She is only for visitors, isn't this what you say for everything? Can't ride the scooter, can't sit on the new sofa, can't eat in the new plates, so how can I go to the new wife!"

Why do you keep everything for others? Keep some for yourself, for your own use. At the moment you have only one life - who knows when death will take away this life and who knows where you will go; only God knows and you are not God. So don't waste time in accumulating things. Enjoy what you have - but with the understanding that objects are insentient, they do not have life. Often family disputes are for material things. You may acquire the desired object but sometimes you end up losing the relationship. Respect the other person, respect yourself and share whatever you have. It is in dire need that a person asks for something. To fulfil his need, the unfortunate person in need has to relinquish his decorum but you don't be brash and brazenly decline to help him.

There is a profound saying by Jesus, "If someone asks for your coat, give him your shirt too." You have so many, what difference will it make to you? Learn to share. I suggest you invite your friends over to your house. If you ask them to come over for meditation, they may refuse saying that you have gone mad. However, if you invite people for dancing, they will accept at once! Let them dance as they wish to, but you don't dance like them. Close your eyes and surrender to God, "This body is your puppet and you are pulling its strings making it dance." Watch yourself dance as a witness. Your friends will be dancing with their eyes open, watching others, dancing to show others. In some time, they will notice you and get intrigued with your dancing. That would be the moment to tell them how to dance with eyes closed and experience the joy. Isn't that what everyone wants – enjoyment, entertainment?

Mantra sadhana is for your solitude; but you can involve your friends and relatives in kirtan and dance - meditation. Life should be disciplined – not the discipline that is imposed on you by others, but the one that you have chosen for yourself. If I ask you to rise at four in the morning, you may find it very difficult, inconvenient and dictatorial. But if you decide that you will get up at four, then it is your own decision and there is no question of dictatorship, instead you will find it delightful.   Here in the ashram you wake up according to the rules of the ashram. At home you rise according to your own sweet will. The day you wake up early of your own free will, you will experience a joy that will be bliss in itself.

Seeker: What is awareness? What is the distinction between awareness and concentration?

Gurumaa: Concentration is attentiveness; having a single-minded focus on something. Let me exemplify this: when you switch on a torch, a beam of light comes out of it and falls on an object. This beam of light is attentiveness, and the energy stored in the cells which make this beam happen, is awareness.

There is a profound difference between awareness and concentration. You may have concentration but no awareness. On the other hand, with awareness one can create concentration and that too whenever and wherever you want it. Nevertheless, to understand and fathom your awareness, concentration can be used as a stepping-stone.

Often people do not possess a clear understanding of the two and confuse awareness with concentration. Awareness is not concentration and concentration is not awareness. The consciousness that makes your mind and brain think and work is awareness, whereas, concentration is just a wave of the mind. It is possible that a person has the concentration but not awareness. You may have seen a goldsmith at work – he uses a blowpipe whilst simultaneously making the finest designs and the prettiest bangles, earrings and necklaces – his hands are involved in a very delicate craft. He has no dearth of concentration. Similarly, watch a painter, an artist - he is totally engrossed in his art.

Air Traffic Control employees also work with great concentration. The controller sits in his tower monitoring each flight that takes off and lands and ensures that the time gap between flights is correct. A single mistake can prove fatal. The distance between two planes, when to turn, when to reduce speed and by how much – all this information is handled by him. This job demands immense concentration. Can a train engine driver do his job without concentration? If his attention flounders, an accident is inevitable. In fact, working in kitchen too requires some degree level of focus. However, delectable food can only be made by those women who possess a good degree of concentration. If not, being forced to eat the insipid and distasteful food will be no less than a punishment! Although, sometimes a couple is so "perfectly compatible" that the husband is as unconscious as the wife – he will be blissfully oblivious of the unappetising and unpalatable food cooked by the wife!

I have observed that fools befriend fools; fools cannot befriend intelligent people. In the same way, an intellectual is likely to have a good rapport with someone of his own calibre. Marriage between an intelligent person and a fool is likely to end up in fights, arguments and rebukes – providing free entertainment to the neighbours!

Without concentration, you cannot even run your business. You have to keep track of your appointments and meetings, or else you will lose out on business deals. Today the situation is such that even when you are meeting someone for a business deal, you need to be well versed about their likes and dislikes. You find out his favourite eating places and the ones he dislikes, his favourite drink, and even whether he has it with soda or with water! You even find out if he is interested in women, and make provisions accordingly! None of this is possible without concentration. In fact, the thefts and cyber crimes that happen are also not possible without concentration.

All possess the ability of concentration, to a greater or lesser level. But awareness, which works at the foundation, is present at a much lesser degree. Often I have noticed that some people are so deficient in concentration that they do not understand even simple things. If you tell them: go straight, first turn to the right and then to the left - they will go straight, first turn to the left instead of right and then curse you!

Mullah Nasruddin was standing in the market square chewing sugarcane. A traveller asked him, "How to get to Jamal Khan's house?" Mullah said that Jamal Khan was his childhood friend, his house was very easy to find and his instructions would get him there in five minutes. Mullah said: "Go straight from here and turn left. A little ahead you will come to a T-junction, from there you turn right and then straight ahead you will see his yellow coloured house."

So the traveller followed Mullah's instructions and came to a yellow house, but this was the same house under which Mullah was standing! The man said to Mullah, "You made me run around in circles. I have landed up where I started. What sort of a person are you?" Mullah replied, "I did not make you run around in circles, I was only testing you to see if you would follow my instructions. Well, right behind me is the house of Jamal Khan!"

I do not have time to waste in imparting knowledge which you are not going to utilise. If you listen to me attentively, I will instruct you further. However, your concentration level is low and you are living your life in such way that it is deteriorating.

I would like to offer a bit of advice on this subject: Although there is nothing wrong in using calculators or computers, but excessive use of calculators lowers concentration. You save telephone numbers in your mobile phones but this too reduces your ability to remember numbers. Those who have crossed 40 or are in their late 30's should definitely stop using a calculator and start using their brains instead! You need to be concerned about your brain and not only your heart. Otherwise, by the time you reach the age of 60-65, your memory begins to fail and slowly diseases like Alzheimer's, dementia and Parkinson's can set in. When you stop using your brain, when you stop challenging it, you can suffer from these diseases - so keep using your brain. Keep up the habit of reading as reading is very necessary. Play intelligent games like chess, which is certainly a good challenge for the mind. Chess sharpens the mind, as you have to think of a move ten times before making it and you not only calculate your moves but also the moves of your opponent. Consequently, you must keep reading something new to stimulate the brain. The more you use your brain, the healthier the neuronal network functions and your memory will improve.

Here is a tip that is surely to improve your memory: In the morning, read any phone number, or better still a verse from a scripture like Gita or Ramayana. Repeat it 3-4 times during the day and then in the evening, try to remember what you had read. Initially, you may not remember or you may forget part of it, but as you continue this practice daily, your capacity to remember will increase.

Life is beautiful, so live it gracefully - don't pollute it. I want to ask you a question: Till now, what all have you created? Remember, producing children is not creativity – they have been accidentally born to you, as a consequence of your copulation. A couple was enjoying each other's body and unknowingly a child was conceived; nothing wrong in that, family grows. But what have you created? What have you conceived? What beauty have you created - a poem, a painting, a song, a game - name something? God has given you a beautiful, resplendent world to live in. Have you enjoyed, appreciated its beauty? Have you added anything to it? If nothing else, plant a few seeds, add some colour! Create something! Painting, dancing, song, music…..be with something that is creative, any one thing that pleases the soul; making money is not creativity.

Fazlu told his friend that he had acquired lot of money; the bag in his hand was full of Rs 500 notes. "Till yesterday you had nothing, you were a pauper. Where did you get so many notes from?" asked the friend. "I hope you are not doing something illicit like drugs or terrorism. Where did you get a bag full of notes from? What's up? What is the true story?" Fazlu replied, "It's nothing of the sort. I just went to the thieves' market and bought fake notes. I got a bag full for Rs 500 notes. See how real they look!" Children play with these fake notes; in schools they are used to teach children the value of money. For example, they are told to calculate how much change is to be taken back for a purchase of Rs 400 worth of goods - if a thousand rupee note is tendered. Our schools are great – even education imparted is related to money! Money is regarded as God. And everyone worships this God. Other than money, is there anything else which motivates you?

Recitation of OM, kirtan, dance, nada yoga and yoga nidra – include these in your daily living and practice regularly. Soon you will realise that yoga nidra is as important as sleeping or eating. Living in the society, all you do is accumulate tension. To remove this stress you must do yoga nidra. In the morning, after a bath, do asana and pranayama followed by recitation of OM mantra or gunjan dhyana.

If you work in an office, you may not have sufficient time to take a break in the afternoon. If possible, do yoga nidra in the morning or when you return home from work. The problem arises if you live in a big city like Delhi or Mumbai. By the time you get home you are so tired that doing yoga nidra at that time means going off to sleep straight away. To do yoga nidra, it is important that your body must not be tired.

If you are tired then maybe do some light asanas, as they would be really relaxing. For example, you have walked a lot during the day and your legs are aching, and you think that on reaching home you will ask your wife or son to massage your legs, but as you reach home and find that both have gone out for some personal work. Now, instead of cursing them or calling them useless, just sit in vajrasana. Folding your knees and sitting with your hips on your heels is the best method to relieve all aches and pains from your legs.

To soothe your tired legs, sitting in a hot bathtub works very well, as water has a great therapeutic value. If you don't have a bathtub, get a large tub in which you can sit, even if your head and feet lie outside. Add a few drops of jasmine or sandalwood oil to it. If it's winter, the water should be warm, and if it's summer then the water should be at room temperature. Quietly sit in the water - you will be so relaxed that all your fatigue will just disappear. Keep breathing deeply and with the breath either do mantra japa, chant any vedic mantra or listen to some soothing music. This will be calming and relaxing. I have just recorded a series of vedic mantras; one of the albums is of mahamrityunjaya mantra. One must know the right way to listen to a mantra, including the pauses in between the words i.e. listen to the gaps too. Mantras have a profound impact on the brain. They affect not only the biochemicals within it but also have a direct effect on the endocrine system.

Magnotherapy can cure diseases. However, magnetic energy is invisible and one can't see the rays emanating from magnets. Similarly, waves of the divine sound of vedic mantras make your body healthy. This also purifies the environment and one can get a whiff of fragrance in the air. Move inwards and listen to the divine sound resonating within, enjoy the bliss.

Light a candle; if possible, light a lamp sometime. Sit with your family and listen to some pleasant music. Close your eyes and witness yourself listening to the music. If you have understood all the important things I have talked about, then you must incorporate them in your life.

Seeker: I have had a valve replacement surgery 10 months ago. Which methodology should I be practicing now?

Gurumaa: I suggest that you practice nadi shodhana along with yoga nidra. I would like to reiterate that in the regular practice of yoga nidra, the time of sankalpa is paramount. Whatever resolve you make at that time will definitely come to fruition. Don't be foolish and ask for your knee problems or your stomach ailments to be cured!

Be more expansive and pragmatic; compose a resolve which is more in unison with your total wellbeing and not just a local problem. The sankalpa should be collective, comprehensive, creative and spiritual.

The statement should be brief, purposeful and resolute. This should be repeated every day and remember that this is not a list of demands – you don't make a new sankalpa everyday! A consistent, unfaltering and determined resolve will definitely fructify. If a patient lying on a hospital bed does yoga nidra, within 2 or 3 days he will feel lighter, rested and relaxed.

I have a disciple in New Jersey who is a neurologist – he runs a very big hospital. I conducted an experiment on yoga nidra there. There was a lady called Barbara who was being treated at this hospital. She suffered from such terrible nightmares that she would become violent and break everything within her reach, so much so that on several occasions she had thrashed her own husband. He had separated from her since last 4 years because when she got nightmares she would lose all control. She didn't know me at all; all she was told was that a new test had been planned for her.

I was present in the hospital monitoring the experiment. Barbara's arm used to shake all the time. Within 20 minutes of starting yoga nidra, her arm stopped shaking. When the session was over, after 42 minutes, she was asked how she felt. She said, "I have never felt so relaxed, so peaceful and calm in my entire life." When I told her that the tremor in her arm had stopped, she could not believe it was possible. When she saw the video recording she was in disbelief and asked the doctor if she could come every day. The doctors had been treating her for long, but to no avail and because of this problem, she was on the verge of a divorce - not because they had any personal differences, but because her problem was destroying her family life. A person who does not sleep all night is bound to be highly irritable.

Yoga nidra has a deep reaching beneficial effect on the body and the mind. In addition to yoga nidra, do practice vipareeta karani asana. Pay attention to your diet and banish the fear of falling ill again from your mind. Affirm that you are in good health – nothing will happen to you. You had a problem, your valve was replaced. Say to yourself that all is well and believe that nothing wrong is going to happen to you.

CHAPTER 8

Asana & Awareness

Asana is the third step of Ashtangayoga. It is primarily related to the body but yoga does not view the body and mind as separate entities. The gross form of the mind is the body and the subtle form of the body is the mind. This is the reason why your mind can be read through your face. The state of mind can be perceived from the movements, gestures and conduct of the body.

As the body and mind are connected, and in fact are one, rishis talked about disciplining the body and hence the science of yogasanas was born. From the point of view of the scriptures, we find a reference to asanas even during the times of Upanishad which is also referred to as vedic times. Lord Shiva was the first to discuss asanas with his consort and disciple Uma.

It is said that when Lord Shiva imparted this knowledge to Uma, twelve of his disciples were also present who memorised and wrote the instructions according to their own intellect and understanding. Thereafter, an organised system of writing the scriptures was developed.

The importance of asanas is mentioned in Bhagawad Gita and Nada Bindu - one of the vedic scriptures and Upanishads. However, this knowledge is disguised mystically in an esoteric language. In the excavations of Mohenjo-Daro and Harappa – home to ancient civilizations – carvings and paintings depicting men and women in various yogic postures have been found.

It is said that there are about 84,000 asanas, but they are not mentioned together in any one scripture. Shiva's teachings on yoga were scattered in tantra, which was kept very secretive, but were finally compiled and presented in a comprehensive manner by Rishi Patanjali. Therefore, we consider his 'yoga sutras' to be the most authentic and complete scripture of Raja Yoga.

Twisting and turning your body erratically is not asana - there is a complete science behind it. Now the question arises, how did the rishis and sages learn it all? The answer to this is 'nature'. Nature was their guru! They studied the behaviour and activities of different animals and realised the benefits of different asanas on different parts of the body. The rishis, therefore, came to know about asanas after diligent observation and contemplation.

It is intriguing to note that even in the absence of the different tools used by modern science like microscope, ultrasound or X-ray, the yogis discovered the precise knowledge about human anatomy - that this body has two lungs, one heart, two kidneys, a gall bladder, a spine; the structure of the brain, the network of nerves, how impulses travel in the entire body and how the brain sends instructions to control various activities, how the sensations of heat and cold are perceived by the body, how are different colours identified - where did the yogis learn about all of this?

In the early days of medical science in the west, dead bodies were dug up at night and dissected in order to study anatomy. It was with great effort that they learnt anatomy. However, this was possible only due to access to dead bodies. Whereas in India digging up the dead body was not an option as most of the religions practiced here namely Buddhism, Jainism, Sikhism or Hinduism, advocate cremation of the dead body.

At one time, the situation was such that people had to appoint a guard for the graveyard, because quite often a grave would be found dug up and the corpse found missing. Scientific researchers wanted to dissect the dead bodies to study the anatomy of internal organs. Even today there must be a huge number of corpses dissected in medical colleges of India to learn human anatomy. The knowledge of anatomy in the Christian and Jewish world is the gift of dead bodies; but in India the dead bodies are mostly burnt, then how was it possible for the rishis of ancient India to understand the human body, the anatomy and the physiology?

It is said that yogis gained this knowledge by using esoteric means. It was through the medium of the pranic body that the yogi could enter his own physical body to study the internal organs. We have three bodies: physical, subtle and causal body. The subtle body and physical body are conjoined by pranic energy. The yogi in this way studied gross organs as well as the intricate and complex network of nerves from head to toe. Initially, this was thought to be a mere conjecture, a gossip, but today western science is coming closer to the realisation that the descriptions of the organs, spine and chakras given by the rishis were not wrong. Today there is scientific evidence of this - rishis observed nature at the external level and gained knowledge of their own bodies from within through subtle ways.

Now let us understand the human body. Which one, do you think, is the most important system in your body? It is the digestive system! This is made up of the digestive tract - a series of hollow organs joined in a long, twisting tube from the mouth to the anus - and other organs that help the body in digesting and metabolising food. Organs that make up the digestive tract are the mouth, oesophagus, stomach, small intestine, large intestine (also called the colon), rectum, and anus; inside these hollow organs is a lining called the mucosa. In the mouth, stomach, and small intestine, the mucosa contains tiny glands that produce juices to help digest food. The digestive tract also contains a layer of smooth muscle that helps break down food and move it along the tract.

Two major digestive organs, the liver and the pancreas, produce digestive juices that reach the intestine through small tubes called ducts. The gall bladder stores the digestive juices synthesised by the liver until they are needed in the intestine. Parts of the nervous and circulatory systems also play major roles in the digestive system.

When you consume food such as bread, meat and vegetables, it is not in a form that the body can use as nourishment. Food must be broken down into small particles before their nutrients can be absorbed into blood and carried to cells throughout the body. Digestion is the process by which food is broken down into smallest parts for the body to build and nourish cells and to provide energy.

How is Food Digested?

Digestion involves breaking and mixing of food with digestive juices, moving it through the digestive tract, and breaking down food into smaller molecules. Digestion begins in the mouth, when you chew and swallow, and the process completes in the small intestine.

The large, hollow organs of the digestive tract contain a layer of muscle that enables their walls to move. The movement propels food and liquid through the system and also mixes the contents. This movement of food is called peristalsis. Peristalsis looks like an ocean wave travelling through the muscle. The muscle of the organ contracts to create a narrowing and then propels the narrowed portion slowly down the length of the organ. These waves push the food and fluid ahead of them through each hollow organ.

Digestion Begins in the Brain

Before taking your meal, you start to imagine how good the food is going to taste. You get an eyeful when you walk past the buffet table at the beginning of the party. Your eyes and your nose get your body and mind in the mood for food, and just the thought of food gets the digestive juices flowing. Your mouth waters, and your stomach churns at the very thought of what is soon to grace your pallet. Even before the first bite you think, sniff, and drool your digestion machine into action. Just anticipating eating gets the intestinal tract ready for the job coming its way.

When the food enters the mouth, your teeth break it down into smaller particles, increasing the surface area through which the chemical food processors - enzymes - can penetrate the food. Next follows the process of chewing that breaks up the fibre that holds the food together and unwraps the food package so that the digestive enzymes can easily access the contents inside. The saliva already flowing in anticipation of eating bathes the broken-down food. Even the fat in the food gets a head start on digestion while it's in the mouth by receiving a tiny squirt of a fat-digesting enzyme called lingual lipase. It is interesting to note that the names of enzymes here are a combination of the suffix 'ase' and the nutrient they work on. For example, lipase digesting lipids, proteinase digesting proteins, and lactase dissolving lactose.

Saliva plays a major role in digestion as it lubricates the food, making that soft peanut butter slip-and-slide down the ten-inch long esophagus, the tube that connects the mouth and the stomach. Saliva is the body's own health juice. Besides helping with digestion, saliva contains a recently-discovered substance called epidermal growth factor (EGF), which facilitates the growth and repair of injured or inflamed intestinal tissue.

Taking smaller bites, chewing the food well, and swallowing slowly are some of the things you can do to better prepare the food package for the next part of its journey. Also, chewing foods slowly slows down your eating. You'll swallow less air (so less burping), and you can be more aware of signals that tell your stomach it's getting full. When each step along the disassembly line is done well, the next job is easier.

Swallowed food is pushed into the oesophagus, which connects the throat above with the stomach below. At the junction of the oesophagus and stomach, there is a ring like muscle, called the gastro-oesophageal sphincter, closing the passage between the two organs. As food approaches the closed sphincter, the sphincter relaxes and allows the food to pass through to the stomach.

The stomach has three mechanical tasks. First, it stores the swallowed food and liquid. To do this, the muscle of the upper part of the stomach relaxes to accept large volumes of swallowed material. The second task is to mix up the food, liquid, and digestive juice produced by the stomach which takes place in the distal part by its muscle action. The third task of the stomach is to empty its contents slowly into the small intestine.

Several factors affect emptying of the stomach, including the kind of food and the degree of muscle action of the emptying stomach and the small intestine. Carbohydrates, for example, spend the least amount of time in the stomach, while protein stays in the stomach longer, and fats stay for the longest. As the food dissolves into the juices from the pancreas, liver, and intestine, the contents of the intestine are mixed and pushed forward to allow further digestion.

Finally, the digested nutrients are absorbed through the intestinal walls into the blood stream and transported throughout the body. The waste products of this process include undigested parts of the food, known as fibre and older cells that have been shed from the mucosa. This is pushed into the colon, where it remains until the faeces are expelled via rectum through the anus.

Like the lungs, other internal organs also need an adequate supply of energy. If there is a dearth of oxygen, then these organs do not function at their optimum capacity, and if they do not function properly, then in spite of eating well, you will remain weak and diseases will affect the body. Rishis have suggested asanas so that sufficient energy can be made available for the functioning of the digestive system.

A perfectly functioning digestive system ensures good health - asanas such as pawanmuktasana, paschimottanasana, bhujangasana, ardhamatsyendrasana, ekpaadchakrasana, dwipaadchakrasana, uttanpaadasana, mandukasana are recommended for good functioning of the digestive system.

Food is an important and integral part of our life - in fact one works and earns for food and may even rob, steal or kill for food. However, if you eat stale, heavy food and do not exercise regularly, the body begins to fall prey to diseases. What you eat is going to be part of your body, so right choice of food is of utmost importance. The body needs combination of protein, carbohydrates, sugar, and minerals. It is not only important to know what you eat, but also whether that gets properly assimilated in the body. If the digestive system is not functioning well, then you may eat the best of food but it will not get assimilated and will get washed out of the body. If your body does not get adequate nourishment, it will become diseased, leading to increased catabolism which in turn can reduce the lifespan and lead to early death.

Yogis have explained that human body is an important vehicle, a tool for spiritual growth. They advised that if your body is not healthy for a prolonged period of time, then you would not even be able to meditate or do any sadhana – so first and foremost, keep your body healthy.

Asanas do not provide health benefits alone. The word asana means: 'kaya sthiram' that which steadies the body (kaya) and one experiences comfort. Have you ever seen anyone perform the shirshasana or mayurasana? In shirshasana, the body is upside down. One needs to train oneself to get right co-ordination and balance to be still and steady as well as comfortable in shirshasana. It is called the king of asanas. One can derive great benefit from this asana as we are always standing on our feet and it is only in this asana that we are on our head and feet are up in air - this sends blood rushing towards head, lungs and all other organs and heart rests because it does not have to work against the gravity to push the blood.

This rush of blood soothes and calms all organs with oxygenated blood and thus ensures perfect functioning of the body. Similarly, sarvangasana is called the queen of asanas. It has a very specific affect on thyroid and parathyroid glands. Every asana has a particular effect on specific organs and muscles. Therefore, one needs to have an in-depth understanding of asanas including the right way to do them.

Since asanas have profound effect on your body, it is important to perform them with awareness. For example, if you are doing leg-raises then you should raise and lower your legs with full awareness, being alert to the action. If you don't move your legs with awareness then it is not asana, it is merely a form of exercise. Asanas should be done with awareness of the body along with breath.

Like in tadasana, you raise your arms straight up while breathing in. When you raise your arms while breathing in, the oxygen reaches all parts of the lungs - posterior, anterior, superior and inferior. When you breathe in without raising your arms, only the upper and to some extent the middle part of the lungs are oxygenated and carbon dioxide accumulates in the rest of the lungs. Carbon dioxide is toxic to the body and the accumulation of toxins is akin to inviting illnesses and early death.

While performing asanas, it is extremely important to keep the mind alert, remain aware, and establish co-ordination with the breath. It is of utmost importance to learn precisely from your teacher (or while referring to a book) when to breathe in and when to breathe out while doing any asana.

Yogis say that if your spine is young, you are young - so to keep your spine young, you should practice all asanas which make the spine flexible and strong. For example, bhujangasana, sarpasana, makarasana, ushtrasana, kandharasana are of utmost importance for the spine. And one should learn them under the guidance of a good yoga practitioner only.

The Spiritual Benefits of Asanas

According to hatha yoga, a major advantage of doing asanas is that they have a direct effect on our chakras - muladhara, manipuraka, swadhisthana, anahata, vishuddha, ajña, sehasrara – thus helping immensely in the awakening of chakras. While doing an asana, when you are breathing in rhythm, it balances the ida and pingala nadi and helps in activating the sushumna nadi. It may seem that you are doing asanas, but actually you are preparing for the awakening of the chakras and the kundalini. If the muladhara and swadhisthana chakras are not activated, a person cannot be free of material and sexual desires, no matter how much theoretical knowledge he gathers by listening to spiritual discourses.

Muladhara chakra controls all the systems related to waste elimination at physical and psychological level and it stores all primal urges.

All your longings and desires are trapped and locked in the swadhisthana chakra. Your thoughts, behaviour, intelligence and nature are under the influence of the swadhisthana. If someone is selfish or short-tempered, it is because of the inactivated swadhisthana. The mechanism of swadhisthana chakra is so subtle that its understanding is beyond the intellect of any average man or woman. Our conscious mind is unaware about how the swadhisthana chakra controls our samskaras – mental impressions, choices, decisions and actions - even your friends are, in a way, selected by the swadhisthana. Currently it is inert and not yet awakened – no one can gain control over the mind and body without activating the swadhisthana chakra.

You have listened to the discourse directing you to give up lust, but since your muladhara is dormant it is but natural that from this unconscious muladhara, three primal urges - sex, sleep and hunger - emerge and you have no control over them. If the swadhisthana chakra is not awakened, then all the knowledge which you have heard just keeps on accumulating somewhere in the corner in the circuits of the brain, but remains unavailable to you. Moreover, if sudden hypertension results in brain haemorrhage, you will lose all this information and all this knowledge.

Many vedantic sages were found unconscious in their last days - they suffered for months, even lost their memory and sense of self-identity. They did not remember whether they were saints or a guru or what..? All throughout their lives they studied and taught 'Vedanta', but just theoretical knowledge can earn followers; such oratory can beget wealth and fame but at the time of disease and death this turns out to be useless, utterly useless. Knowledge remains stored in some of the brain cells - one blood vessel ruptures, cells are destroyed and all the accumulated knowledge goes in vain - end of story! Without the foundation of yoga - without yama, niyama, asana, pranayama, etc. – bookish knowledge is not worth a penny!

Dhyana (meditation) is distinct from Dharana (attentiveness)

If the body cells are not healthy, glandular secretions are not normal and oxygen inhaled is not adequate, then it is impossible to have deep concentration and focus. What you assume to be concentration is probably tandra and whenever you think that you are in deep meditation, it is actually a state of tandra or semi-unconsciousness. You lose account of time and feel good but it is just a deep dark unproductive zone. Don't you feel good while you are asleep!

The person, who enters the stage of dhyana directly without going through the stages of asana and pranayama, faces the same problem which most of you are facing. You want to meditate but you cannot; you want to still your mind but you are not able to; and sometimes when you feel your mind is still, are you sure that you were not unconscious and that you were fully aware? Who will know this? When you close your eyes and the thoughts settle down a bit and the mind relaxes, the tendency of the mind is to go into sleep – this tendency is not new but is several lifetimes old. It is very difficult for the mind to be still and alert.

What is the state of meditation? This has been defined in yoga, so that you know whether you are in a state of meditation or concentration. Often people confuse the two, but they are distinct. Those who practice meditation often pat themselves on the back saying that they have experienced bliss – well that happens in concentration too. What yardstick do you have to judge whether your bliss was the result of concentration or some deeper state of awareness?

The entire personality changes when meditation happens! You think that you are making a few mistakes, but largely you are right and you need to fix only a few things here and there. To a large extent you think you are a good person who is on the right track. You justify your mistakes by thinking - so what? Everyone has shortcomings! So you do self-glorification that you are better than many others. Mind well, this is your ego! See how people fool themselves - they think they have only a few attachments, everything else is fine; some anger is left, else is fine; just a little pleasure lies in food, else it's fine! No, this is not true. What seems to be partially wrong is in fact completely wrong. When you will rectify it totally, only then will you be completely free. If you want success in meditation, you need sound foundation of yama, niyama, asana and pranayama.

Effects of Yoga on the Body

A yoga practitioner has a well developed pineal gland. The pineal gland is a small endocrine gland in the vertebrate brain. It produces melatonin, a hormone that affects the modulation of wake/sleep patterns and photoperiodic (seasonal) functions. It is shaped like a tiny pinecone and is located near to the centre of the brain, between the two hemispheres, tucked in a groove where the two rounded thalamic bodies join. The secretion activity of the pineal gland has only recently been understood. Historically, its location deep in the brain indicated to philosophers that it possessed a particular importance.

In yogic science it is called the ajña chakra - the third eye. The pineal gland is cone-shaped, about the size of a pea, and is in the centre of the brain in a tiny cave, behind and above the pituitary gland, which lies a little behind the root of the nose. It is located directly behind the eyes, in vicinity of the third ventricle.

The true function of this mysterious gland has long been contemplated by philosophers and spiritual adepts. Ancient Greeks believed the pineal gland to be our connection to the realms of thought. Descartes called it the seat of the soul.

This gland is activated by light, and it controls the various biorhythms of the body. It works in harmony with the hypothalamus, which controls the body's thirst, hunger, sexual desire, and the biological clock that determines our aging process.

When the pineal gland awakens, one may feel a pressure at the base of the brain. This pressure will often be experienced when connecting to a higher frequency.

When one practices a special technique called 'bhuchari', it activates the pineal gland. Bhuchari can be learnt from a master and can be easily mastered. Amongst pranayama, nadi shodhana has a direct effect on the pineal gland.

The hypothalamus, pineal and pituitary glands are not very big in size, yet any dysfunction of these leads to a breakdown of all bodily systems. What is the role of hypothalamus in human body? In the fairly large human body, this is like a small chip shaped computer. The pituitary and pineal glands communicate with each other in signals which are further decoded by the hypothalamus. According to this decoded information, the hypothalamus influences various endocrine glands to secrete hormones – the chemical messengers which play an important role in various bodily functions, for example, growth, development, metabolism, etc. If the hormones are removed from the human body, nothing will be left behind. The fact is that these three small glands - pituitary, hypothalamus and pineal are responsible for the biggest task i.e. normal functioning of the whole body.

Some asanas have a direct influence on these glands and thus their dysfunctions can be corrected. With sarvangasana you can keep these important glands in excellent working order. If the body can be held in the sarvangasana for 10 minutes, blood flow to the brain increases considerably. However, you will be able to do this only by consistent and regular practice. Sarvangasana literally means a pose for all the parts of the body. It is one of the many inverted poses of yoga, all of which are extremely beneficial. These inverted asanas work by reversing the effects of gravity on certain parts of the body, and in sarvangasana most parts of the body are targeted. Sarvangasana helps promote good circulation, as it directs the blood flow of the entire lower body towards the heart. This asana also helps prevent and reduce varicose veins by reducing the pressure on the legs and directing the blood clogged in the veins upwards to the heart.

Inverted yogasanas also direct oxygen to the upper lung, ensuring healthier lungs. Usually the heart has to work hard to ensure that blood gets pushed upward to the brain. During sarvangasana the heart gets a relief as the blood is directly relayed to the brain.

The second most important asana is shirshasana. The longer the time you can hold the posture for, the greater are its benefits. This is in fact true for every asana especially when you awarefully co-ordinate the postures with breath. This results in greater availability of pranic energy to all the important glands.

Deep breathing for a longer period means increased oxygenation of the blood and increased release of unwanted carbon dioxide by the tissue cells which is exhaled out of the body. When we breathe, thanks to gravity, our lower lungs get most of the oxygen while our upper lungs don't. It's only when we take a deep breath that our upper lungs too get some oxygen. When you inhale, the air reaches the lungs via nasal passages and wind pipe. Within the lungs there are small sacs called alveoli where the gas exchange takes place - oxygen from the inhaled air is released and carbon dioxide from blood comes out via the exhaled breath.

The thyroid gland is shaped like a butterfly, having wings on left and right side, located in the throat region of neck. Over a period of time due to lack of adequate circulation of oxygenated blood, the function of this gland starts to deteriorate. The regular practise of Sarvangasana strengthens the thyroid gland.

When you do sarvangasana, the chin touches the chest and exerts pressure on neck where the thyroid gland is located. The thyroid gland gets oxygenated blood that nourishes thyroid and gradually it begins to function normally; hence the secretion of T3, T4 and TSH hormones gets balanced. Thyroid gland controls metabolism of the body. Metabolism is the composite of catabolism – process of breaking larger molecules into smaller ones releasing energy, and anabolism – process of synthesis creating complex molecules from simpler ones.

Thyroid dysfunction leads to an imbalance of T3, T4 and TSH levels. If the thyroid gland overworks, it leads to a condition called hyperthyroidism – the body becomes emaciated and the skin becomes dry. There is excessive hunger, but no amount of food seems to nourish the patient. It also leads to increase in allergies, physical weakness, loss of hair and the immune system becomes suppressed.

If the thyroid function is suppressed, then it leads to a disease called hypothyroidism, and in this case the reverse symptoms occur – the body swells up and gets bloated, the patient experiences extreme lack of energy leading to lethargy, the process of digestion is disrupted and the sleep pattern gets disturbed. Lack of proper sleep causes dysfunction of the pineal, pituitary and hypothalamus because they work at their optimum when we are asleep. All the hormones necessary for a healthy body are secreted in the night, so sleeping on time is important for good health.

Some days you sleep at 10 O' clock, some days at 12 am at night, or at 2 am. You are eating, drinking, gossiping, watching a movie, roaming around, reading, possibly a spiritual book! – all this is harmful because it denies the body much needed rest. How will the body then secrete the required hormones optimally at the right time? As a result, you will become prone to diseases and end up not enjoying either the world or spirituality.

The thyroid gland controls metabolism, absorption of nutrients from food and the entire process of digestion. Just below the thyroid is the parathyroid gland. Its function is tremendously enhanced by sarvangasana, matsyasana and setubandhasana. If a thyroid patient practices asanas like halasana and suptamatsyasana for a prolonged period of time, his parathyroid dysfunction will get rectified. Halasana and sarvangasana are beneficial in correcting the thyroid function. The pineal and pituitary glands send instructions to the thyroid and parathyroid glands which work in conjunction with each other; these instructions are analysed by the hypothalamus which in turn influences hormonal secretions affecting sleep, digestive capacity, etc.

Just above the kidneys are the adrenal glands which secrete adrenaline. Adrenaline controls the 'fight or flight' reaction of the body. When faced with danger, in a fraction of a second the hypothalamus instructs the entire body to protect itself by issuing the 'fight or flight' instruction. For example, if you are facing a wild beast or an enemy, you will try to escape – run away! You will not stop to contemplate on your options, will you? In this way, adrenaline, the hormone secreted by the adrenal directs you to take the appropriate action – this is the control that nature has given you.

Adrenaline is also secreted when you get angry. It is not required though as you do not need to run away from danger, but anger does lead to the desire to inflict hurt. When the person you are having an argument with is stronger, then you might want to escape. So adrenal gland becomes activated and adrenaline gets secreted. Let's suppose, you go to someone's house burning in anger, ready to fight, but you find the house locked. There is a rush of adrenaline and your whole body is tense, your muscles are tense. At the gate, a huge Alsatian dog is barking ferociously. Your instinct tells you to run or else the dog will tear you to shreds. You return home with your tail between your legs, not having uttered a word. Good! That was sensible! However, what about the adrenaline that has already been released into your blood stream? Well, that will have its effect.

Say the situation took a turn - you went in anger but came back without having said a word. But the body cannot escape the damage caused by the unnecessary rush of adrenaline. Therefore, it is important that the adrenal function remains normal. For this you will have to keep a cool head and do asanas like paschimottanasana, janushirasana, pawanmuktasana, shashankasana, mandukasana, mayurasana, dhanurasana, ardhamatsyendrasana, chakrasana, shalabhasana, bhujangasana, sarpasana and ushtrasana. With these asanas, our abdomen gets compressed thus normalising the functioning of adrenal.

Women have two ovarian glands, one on either side of the uterus - these ovaries secrete the female hormones. When a woman reaches the age of menopause, the ovaries stop producing the egg or ovum. A child is conceived when the ovum is fertilised by the sperm. If there is a malfunction of the ovaries, post-menopause or pre-menopause, the woman's entire body system gets disturbed leading to weight gain, irritability, disturbed sleep and other ailments. In certain cases, where partial hysterectomy is done wherein one ovary has been removed or in case of total hysterectomy, the health comes under strain. In any case, health can be protected by practicing asana and pranayama regularly as this will enhance total wellbeing.

The ovaries play a very important role in the female body. In the male, the gonads produce testosterone. Testosterone is what makes a man a man - its secretion is more in males. In women, the menstrual cycle usually continues up to the age of 45 or 50; in some cases it may go on till the age of 50 - 52. Slowly the cycle recedes and ultimately the ovaries stop working altogether. The two important hormones produced by the ovary are progesterone and oestrogen, and when their production is reduced, the levels of testosterone start rising. The female starts developing secondary sexual characteristics of the male in both body and temperament namely, coarseness of skin, facial hair and aggression.

As it happens with women, age related changes take place in men too; between the age of 45 and 55 the testosterone levels fall. As men age, they develop feminine qualities like they argue less and remain calm. With age, men mellow down and there seems to be a role reversal with their wives, not because of age, but due to a change in the glandular function of pituitary, hypothalamus, thyroid, parathyroid and adrenal etc.

To reiterate, it is the secretion system that keeps the body fit. If any one gland – thyroid, pineal, hypothalamus, pituitary, adrenal, ovary, and testes start to malfunction, the entire body system will collapse.

The glands perform vital functions therefore your yoga practice should include asanas which strengthen and improve the function of the three glands in the brain, two in the throat, many small ones in intestines, adrenal, ovaries and testes. If even one gland does not function properly, not only will the body be unhealthy, but the mind too will suffer ill health.

The human body is a unique creation; every aspect of it is crafted to perfection. The shape, size and function of each part is well-defined and specific. It is because of the shield of the skin that we cannot see into our body. But the fact is that if the skin is removed and the muscles separated, it won't be a pretty sight!

Our body is a curious entity. When you eat something, food goes down into the food pipe and then into the stomach. Here the food is churned and then it moves into small intestine where nutrients are absorbed and waste matter finally is pushed into large intestine, which finally comes out of anus. Well, no one is concerned about what happens inside the body as all your concern is centred at the tongue alone.

It is the tongue that tastes the food, yet the food does not stay in the mouth for long. You eat more because the food does not stay in your mouth for long and you are not able to satiate the taste buds, hence you end up eating more and more! You forget that the stomach does not relish taste, and in your greed you end up bingeing and upsetting your stomach. The stomach is an elastic organ - its size and capacity can be increased or decreased.

If you see a dissected stomach, you will feel revulsion. What a dirty body! What filth it contains! Gurbani says: Body is a cage made of bones, muscles and nerves, and in it resides a poor bird 'prana'. This body is nothing but a cage made up of bones and muscles in which a poor soul is trapped.

First, one must understand the body and its physical make-up. Then one should lay a firm foundation on the basis of the aspects that will help you live a healthy and meaningful life like requisite discipline, appropriate diet, necessary rest and relaxation. This will help you live a balanced, healthy and controlled life.

The three main glands of the body are in the head and therefore the seat of awareness is also in the brain, which is the chief of all organs present in the body. That is why there is this tradition of prostrating at the feet of the guru. It is a mark of surrender to the master – it is also said that when head is placed close to the master's feet, disciple automatically receives abundance of vibrations from the master, which will help him to evolve spiritually.

Recently, an experiment was conducted in which magnetic impulses were applied to the right side of a person's brain. For the next one hour, this man experienced awakening of artistic talents that did not exist earlier. Before the experiment he was asked to sketch a horse - his horse looked like neither a donkey nor a bull! He was asked to read out a sentence in which a word had been repeated. When he read the sentence, he read the repeated word only once and not twice as was written i.e. he could not even read the written material properly. After the application of magnetic impulses for 15 minutes, he felt strong pulsations in his lips, chin and cheeks.

After 15 minutes the magnets were removed. Now he read the same sentence correctly; even his sketch of a horse - with fine detailing of the face - resembled a horse. However, this effect lasted for only one hour. After one hour he was back to his normal self.

What does this imply? There are some vibrations that can improve the working capacity of the brain. The function of the brain, if abnormal, can be corrected; poor memory can be improved; artistic talents can be awakened! This is possible even in people lacking them. The scientists used magnets, but in the Indian tradition we use dharana and sound vibrations.

In fact, when you do trataka (either with open or closed eyes), OM gunjan or especially pranayama, then by means of dharana and concentration, your brain receives vibrations that are far superior to magnetic impulses. This indicates that the regular practice of these techniques can improve your intellectual capabilities.

Description of Asanas

For the reference of the reader, some asanas are detailed below. These asanas affect the entire working of the body and help strengthen and normalise all functions. If you are a first timer, it is suggested that you learn under the guidance of a trained teacher to begin with.

Precautionary Note: The readers should exercise all precautions before following any of the practices or asanas. To avoid any problems while doing the asanas or following any practice, it is advised that you consult a doctor and a good yoga instructor. The responsibility lies solely with the reader and not with the publication, or the author.

❋ Suryanamaskara (Sun Salutation)

This asana involves 12 different postures. It helps in increasing flexibility of the body and mind. Twelve different postures affect the spine in different ways, requiring proper co-ordination of inhalation and exhalation. Therefore, one feels very peaceful while doing this asana. It should ideally be practised in the beginning of a yoga session.

Method

1. Pranamasana (Prayer Pose)

Stand erect with the feet together and the hands by the sides. Distribute your weight evenly on both feet; find your centre. Breathing naturally, bring both the hands to the chest and fold them in the style of Indian greeting.

2. Hasta Utthanasana (Raised Arms Pose)

Bring the hands down. Raise the arms above the head; the elbows remain locked. Extend the spine backwards, arching the back from the lumber and moving the hips forward; the knees remain locked. Let the eyes follow the hands while relaxing your neck. In this pose, please ensure that you do not hold your breath. Do not stay in this pose for long.

3. Padahastasana (Hand to Foot Pose)

Bend forward from the lumbar and place the palms on the floor besides each foot. The knees should remain locked – make sure you do not bend them. If you cannot touch the ground, then let your hands go only as far as they can, otherwise use props.

4. Ashwa Sanchalanasana (Equestrian Pose)

Now putting the weight on the palms, lunge the left leg behind like a stick, resting on the toes. Bend the left knee and place it on the floor; support weight on both hands, right foot, left knee and toes of the left foot. Lift the head and neck first up and then back. Roll the eyes up. The right foot remains between the hands.

Note: When you repeat this asana, lunge the right leg behind with left leg in the front. You may also want to do some experimentation to determine the comfortable distance to step forward so that you can perform step 4 and 5 in a rhythm.

5. Parvatasana (Mountain Pose)

Bring the right foot back in line with the left.

Simultaneously, raise the buttocks and lower the head between the arms so that the lower portion and the upper portion of  the body form two sides of a triangle. Try and ensure that the heels touch the ground. If you cannot touch your head to the ground, then let it go only as far as it can.

6. Ashtanga Namaskara (Salute with Eight Limbs Pose)

Ashtanga means eight limbs and namaskara means paying homage. In this posture, put the knees down first and then bring the chest down. See that eight parts of the body are touching the floor - two feet, two knees, two hands, the chest and the forehead. Make sure the hips are slightly raised above the ground. Keep the feet together.

7. Bhujangasana (Cobra Pose)

Lower the pelvis and abdomen to the floor. Raise your head slowly up, arch the spine and neck and look up.

Keep your legs together, the elbows straight alongside the body and keep the shoulders down.

8. Parvatasana (Mountain Pose)

Wiggle your toes forward allowing your feet to rest on the soles while you raise the hips as you did in posture 5.

9. Ashwa Sanchalanasana (Equestrian Pose)

Bring the right foot forward and assume posture 4 exactly as before.

10. Padahastasana (Hand to Foot Pose)

Bring the left foot forward. This is the same as posture 3.

11. Hasta Uttanasana (Raised Arms Pose)

Stretch up in a standing pose with your arms up and bend backwards This is the same as posture 2.

12. Pranamasana (Prayer Pose)

Stand erect, bringing the hands back to the centre of the chest with palms together. This is the same as posture 1.

This series of twelve asanas forms one round of suryanamaskara. In the second round, in pose 4, stretch your right leg backwards. Each cycle comprises of two rounds. Always ensure that suryanamaskara is done for an even number of rounds. After each round, you should be in the same spot as started.

Repetitions

In the beginning, repeat the cycle twice or thrice; then slowly, as per your capacity, go on increasing the number of repetitions.

Benefits

Suryanamaskara is a complete physical exercise in itself. Its benefits are not restricted to any single body part - the entire body is affected. Some of the important benefits are given below:

1. It improves the entire endocrine system and regulates the functioning of endocrine glands.

2. Suryanamaskara promotes blood circulation and stimulates the respiratory system in the body.

3. The combination of backward and forward movements in this asana ensures that your digestive system works well. Thus, this asana helps in curing constipation and other digestion-related ailments.

4. For those suffering from insomnia, suryanamaskara is the best medicine.

5. Besides keeping one stress free, suryanamaskara helps in rejuvenating the mind because it promotes the circulation of fresh oxygen to the brain.

6. This balances the transition period between childhood and adolescence in growing children.

Precautions

1. People suffering from high blood pressure, coronary artery disease or those who have had a stroke should avoid this asana.

2. This asana should also be avoided in case of hernia or intestinal tuberculosis.

3. The practice of suryanamaskara should be immediately discontinued in case of fever, acute inflammation, boils or rashes. These may develop due to excess toxins in the body. When the toxins have been eliminated, the practice may be resumed.

4. People suffering from back conditions such as slipped disc and sciatica should not practise this asana.

5. Women should not do the suryanamaskara during menstruation.

6. Pregnant women should not do it after the third month of gestation. Following child-birth, it may be commenced approximately forty days after delivery for re-toning the uterine muscles.

❊ PASCHIMOTTANASANA (INTENSE DORSAL STRETCH)

Most people spend the day on their feet - this leads to a great deal of stress on the spine. Regular practice of the forward bending asanas keeps the spine and joints supple and flexible, thus, internal organs are harmonised and the nadi mandal gets strengthened. To do this asana correctly, it is important that it is done effortlessly without exerting any force on the body. Do this asana after the backward bending asanas.

Method

1. Sit erect with your legs together, stretched out in front of you. Point both feet straight up towards the ceiling.

2. Stretch your arms straight up, touching the ears. Keeping the spine erect, legs straight and knees locked, bend forward from the hips.

3. As far as possible, try to touch the chest to the thighs and the forehead to the knees or beyond. Beginners should bend only as far as they can comfortably.

4. For this posture, try to avoid a lot of curvature in the middle part of the spine.

5. Try to grab the toes with both hands.

6. Breathing normally, hold the pose for 30 seconds.

7. Bring the body back to the starting position.

8. The knees should be locked throughout the practice of this asana.

9. Repeat this asana twice or thrice.

Benefits

1. The muscles of the abdomen, pelvic region including the liver, pancreas, spleen, kidneys and adrenal glands are all toned up and remain healthy.

2. This asana helps alleviate disorders of the uro-genital system.

3. It stimulates circulation to the nerves and muscles of the spine.

4. It is the best therapy for the management of prolapse, menstrual disorders, sluggish liver, diabetes, colitis, kidney complaints, bronchitis and eosinophilia.

Precautions

1. People who suffer from slipped disc should not practice paschimottanasana.

2. Under no circumstance should you force the body into any position. Patients of chronic arthritis, sciatica, back pain should not practice this asana unless and until instructed by a good yoga instructor.

❈ SARVANGASANA (SHOULDER STAND)

Sarvangasana or shoulder stand is an inverted asana in hatha yoga and considered as the 'queen' of asanas. Its literal translation in sanskrit means 'posture of the complete body' and coveys its great significance and stature.

Method

1. Lie on your back keeping the hands by your sides, palms facing upwards and feet together.

2. Rest the back on the ground. Raise both the legs to an angle of 90 degrees.

3. Support the back with both hands and keep raising your hip and back till the body rests on the shoulders. The chin should rest between the clavicle bones.

4. Breathing normally, hold the pose for 30 seconds.

5. Gradually add 5 to 10 seconds every day until you can comfortably hold the pose for 3 or more minutes.

6. To come down, bend your knees into your torso, and roll your back slowly onto the floor, keeping the back of your head on the floor all the while. Take care to come down carefully and smoothly, without jerks and stops.

Note: It is recommended to do this asana before halasana.

Benefits

1. By pressing the chest against the chin, this asana harmonises the thyroid function. Thyroid gland is located in the throat and provides energy to the body, controlling metabolism.

2. This asana balances the circulatory, digestive, reproductive, nervous and endocrine systems.

3. Bringing adequate blood supply to the brain, this asana relieves mental and emotional stress, fear and headaches, and helps clear psychological disturbances.

4. Its influence on the parathyroid glands ensures normal development and regeneration of the bones, preventing premature calcification.

5. Besides massaging the abdominal organs, sarvangasana releases the normal gravitational pressure from the anal muscles, relieving haemorrhoids.

6. Flexibility of the neck vertebrae is improved and the nerves passing through the neck to the brain are toned.

7. Sarvangasana is considered a good yoga therapy for the treatment of asthma, diabetes, colitis, thyroid disorders, impotence, hydrocele,

prolapse, menopause, menstrual disorders and leucorrhoea.

8. This asana helps prevent cough, cold and flu if practiced regularly.

Precautions

1. This asana should not be practiced by those suffering from an enlarged thyroid gland or goitre.

2. Do not practice this asana in case of diarrhoea, high blood pressure, menstruation, neck injury, liver dysfunction, spleen disorder, cervical spondylitis or thrombosis.

3. Do not attempt this asana if you have breathing difficulties or pain in the upper spine.

4. It should be avoided during advanced stages of pregnancy.

❀ HALASANA (PLOUGH POSE)

This asana is recommended to be done after sarvangasana. There is a strong forward stretch exerted on the spine, which makes the entire body supple.

Method

1. First be in sarvangasana posture. Supporting the back with the hands, take the legs behind the head.

2. Bring the toes to the ground.

3. If you cannot touch the ground with your toes, keep supporting the back with your hands so that the back muscles are not strained.

4. As much as possible, keep your torso perpendicular to the floor and your legs fully extended.

5. Beginner should hold this position for 15 seconds.

6. To exit the asana, lift back into sarvangasana, then roll down onto your back.

Note: If any stress is felt while doing sarvangasana or halasana, bend the knees to touch the forehead. Supporting the back with the hands, take a deep breath. After this you are ready for a repetition.

Benefits

1. Halasana massages all the internal organs, activates the digestion, relieving constipation and dyspepsia.

2. Besides revitalising the spleen, this asana promotes the production of insulin by the pancreas and improves liver and kidney function.

3. It improves the functioning of the abdominal organs besides relieving spasms in the back muscles, toning the spinal nerves and increasing blood circulation to the whole area.

4. As the chin presses on the neck, the thyroid gland is massaged. As a result, this asana regulates the activities of the thyroid gland leading to balance in the body's metabolic rate.

5. It stimulates the thymus gland, boosting the immune system.

6. For those having asthma, bronchitis, constipation, hepatitis, urinary tract or menstrual disorders, this asana is a great therapy.

Precaution

Those suffering from hernia, slipped disc, sciatica, high blood pressure or arthritis of the neck should not practise this asana.

✳ VAJRASANA (DIAMOND POSE)

Kneel down and sit back on your heels. The first toe of both the feet should touch each other.

Method

1. Bending the legs at the knees, sit on the knees.

2. The feet should be placed under the hips in such a way that one big toe touches the other.

3. The knees should be together and the heels apart.

4. Rest on the heels.

5. Place the hands on the knees.

Benefits

1. This asana gives you control over your sexual desire. While sitting in vajrasana, there is a direct pressure on the vajra naadi, which controls the sex organs.

2. Sitting in vajrasana is extremely beneficial for the digestive system. This asana greatly helps in relieving stomach ailments such as hyperacidity and peptic ulcer.

3. Vajrasana is beneficial for the abdominal organs.

4. It is also a very good posture for meditation as the spine becomes erect with no effort and it also affects the chakras, e.g. muladhara.

5. This asana is especially beneficial if done after meals as it has a direct effect on digestion. Sit in this asana for as long as you can.

6. Vajrasana alters the flow of blood and nervous impulses in the pelvic region and strengthens the pelvic muscles.

7. It is a preventive measure against hernia and also helps to relieve piles.

8. It assists women in labour and helps alleviate menstrual disorders.

Precautions

1. One should not put more than normal pressure on the arms and the ankle joints while doing this asana.

2. The person should not practice this asana if he/she is suffering from knee injuries.

3. In the beginning if any ankle pain is felt while practising this asana, release the posture, sit with the legs stretched forward and shake the feet vigorously one after the other until the stiffness disappears. Then resume the posture.

4. A folded blanket or small cushion may be placed between the buttocks and the heels for added comfort.

Method

1. Lie flat on your back.

2. Keep both the feet together and hands by the side touching the body.

3. Raise the left leg as high as is comfortable, keeping it straight and slowly lower it. Repeat with the right leg.

4. Start with five rounds and increase up to ten rounds.

Benefit

This asana exercises the muscles of the waist and back and strengthens the digestive system.

Method

1. Lie flat on the back and raise both the legs.

2. As far as possible, keep the legs straight. Do not bend the knees and hold for a few seconds. Slowly lower the legs.

3. Start with five rounds and increase up to ten rounds.

Benefits

1. Raising the legs strengthens muscles of the lower abdomen and waist.

2. As it increases stamina, this asana facilitates the practise of other asanas.

Note: Whenever you do these asanas, ensure that the back rests flat on the ground and the neck and shoulders are stress-free. Ensure that the legs are straight and comfortable, especially when raised.

✿ BADDHAKONASANA (BOUND ANGLE)

Method

1. Sit with your legs straight out in front of you.

2. Bend your knees and pull your heels toward your pelvis.

3. Drop your knees out to the sides and press the soles of your feet together.

4. Try to bring your heels as close to your pelvis as you comfortably can. With the first and second finger and thumb, grasp the big toe of each foot.

5. Always keep the outer edges of the feet firmly on the floor.

6. Never force your knees down. Instead release the heads of the thigh bones toward the floor. When this action leads, the knees follow.

7. Stay in this pose anywhere from 1 to 5 minutes.

8. Then inhale, lift your knees away from the floor, and extend the legs back to their original position.

Benefits

1. This asana stimulates abdominal organs, ovaries and prostate gland, bladder, and kidneys.

2. It is an excellent asana for women in preparation for child birth.

3. It is also very helpful in menopause.

4. This asana stimulates the heart and improves general circulation.

5. It stretches the inner thighs, groin and knees.

6. Practice of this asana soothes menstrual discomfort and sciatica.

7. It is said to be therapeutic for flat feet, high blood pressure, infertility, and asthma.

8. Besides, this asana is very useful in boosting immunity.

Precautions

1. This pose is usually contraindicated for women who have recently given birth.

2. In case of groin or knee injury, place folded blankets or bolsters under your knees for support.

❋ TITALI ASANA (BUTTERFLY POSE)

Method

1. Sit on the floor with both legs spread in front. Keep your head, neck and spine erect.

2. Hold the ankles of the respective legs; bending the legs at the knee, bring the feet closer to the body. Make sure that the outer edge of the feet touch the ground.

3. Firmly grab the big toes pulling the heels towards your body. Flexing the thighs, press the

knees to the ground; keep looking ahead.

4. Push the thighs down with the hands to touch the knees to the ground.

5. Do not apply too much force to ground your knees. Instead, release the heads of the thighbones towards the floor. When this action leads, the knees follow.

6. Now remove the hands from the thighs and hold the feet together. Move the knees up and down without any support. Do not lean in front or back while performing the pose. Continue flapping initially for 20 to 30 times.

Benefits

1. Prepares the legs for padmasana and other meditative asanas.

2. Relieves the inner thigh muscles tension.

3. Removes tiredness from long hours of standing and walking.

4. Helps in relieving stress and lifting your spirits.

5. It is also beneficial to tone the uro-genital system.

Precaution

Sciatica patients and people with knee pain should avoid this yoga pose.

✳ BHUJANGASANA (COBRA POSE)

The name of this asana comes from the sanskrit words bhujanga (snake, serpent) and asana (pose).

Method

1. Lie flat on the stomach with the legs straight, feet together, toes pointing away from the body.

2. Place the palms of the hands flat on the floor, below and slightly to the side of the shoulders.

3. The arms should be positioned so that the elbows point backward and are close to the sides of the body.

4. Without lifting the navel from the floor, raise the chest and head, arching the back.

5. Stretch your body as much as possible.

6. To return to the starting position, slowly bring the head forward, release the upper back by bending the arms, lower the navel, chest, shoulders & finally the forehead to the floor. Relax the lower back muscles.

Benefits

1. This asana is beneficial in relocating slipped disc.

2. It removes backache and keeps the spine supple and healthy.

3. By arching the spine, this asana improves circulation in the back region and toning of the nerves, thus promoting better communication between the brain and body.

4. This asana is especially beneficial for women. It regulates the menstrual cycle, curing problems of irregular menstrual cycles. The reproductive organs are massaged benefiting the ovaries and uterus.

5. It is very beneficial for all the abdominal organs - liver, kidneys etc. It improves appetite and relieves constipation.

6. The adrenal glands are also massaged and stimulated to work more efficiently.

Precaution

If you suffer from stomach ulcer, hernia, intestinal disorders or hyperthyroidism, then this asana should be practised only under the guidance of an able yoga teacher.

❋ DHANURASANA (BOW POSE)

Method

1. Lie flat in prone (face down) position on the floor.

2. Rest the chin on the floor; keep the legs straight and the feet together.

3. Bend the knees and bring the heels close to the buttocks.

4. Clasp the hands around the ankles.

5. Arch the back, lifting the thighs, chest and head together; keep the arms straight.

6. In the final position the head is tilted back and the abdomen supports the entire body on the floor.

7. Hold this pose for about 20 to 30 seconds and then, slowly relaxing the leg muscles, lower the legs, chest and head to the starting position.

8. Release the pose and relax in the prone position until the breath becomes normal.

Benefits

1. The entire alimentary canal is reconditioned by this asana.

2. It massages the liver and the abdominal organs.

3. The pancreas and adrenal glands are toned, thus balancing their secretions.

4. The kidneys are massaged and excess weight is reduced around the abdominal area.

5. This asana leads to improved functioning of the digestive, eliminative and reproductive organs and helps to remove gastro-intestinal disorders, dyspepsia, chronic constipation and sluggishness of the liver.

6. For those suffering from diabetes, incontinence, colitis, menstrual disorders, this asana is a blessing.

7. It improves blood circulation. Dhanurasana is also useful for relieving various chest ailments, including asthma, and for freeing nervous energy in the cervical and thoracic sympathetic nerves, thus improving respiration.

Precautions

1. People who suffer from weak heart, high blood pressure, hernia, peptic or duodenal ulcers should not attempt this practice.

2. Since this asana stimulates the adrenal glands and the sympathetic nervous system, this asana should not be practised before sleep at night.

❈ MATSYASANA (FISH POSE)

The Fish Pose is traditionally performed with the legs in the lotus pose, padmasana. Since padmasana is generally difficult for beginners, here we will work with the legs straight, pressed against the floor.

Method

1. Lie on your back on the floor with legs straight and feet on the floor.

2. Place the hands underneath the buttocks, palms facing down. Bring the elbows closer toward each other.

3. Lift the head and chest up.

4. Keeping the chest lifted up, lower the head backward and bring the crown of the head to the floor.

5. Keeping the head lightly on the ground, press the elbows firmly into the ground and lift your chest up between the shoulder blades. Press

thighs and legs to the floor.

6. Hold this pose and relax.

7. Lift the head up, bring the hands out, and lower the chest and head to the floor.

Benefits

1. This asana stretches the intestines and abdominal organs and is useful for all abdominal ailments.

2. Re-circulating stagnant blood in the back, this asana alleviates backache and cervical spondylitis.

3. This asana helps boost the immune system as it regulates and stimulates the function of thyroid gland and thymus gland respectively.

4. To remove constipation, drink 3 glasses of water and practise this asana.

5. This helps prevent and remove disorders of the reproductive system.

6. As this asana encourages deep respiration, it is a boon for patients of asthma and bronchitis.

Precautions

1. This asana should not be performed by those having high or low blood pressure.

2. People having migraine and those suffering from insomnia should avoid this asana.

3. It is also advised that in case of serious lower-back or neck injuries, one must consult a good yoga practitioner before doing this asana.

4. Pregnant women should not perform this asana.

✳ Ushtrasana (Camel Pose)

Method

1. For this, first sit in vajrasana - resting the hips on the feet with spine erect.

2. Then, stand on your knees keeping a distance of six inches in between your knees and feet.

3. Lean backwards; slowly catch hold of the right heel with the right hand and the left heel with the left hand.

4. Bend from your lumber region.

5. Push the abdomen forward while thighs remain vertical.

6. Bend the head and spine backward as far as possible.

7. Return to the starting position by slowly releasing the hands from the heels, one at a time.

Benefits

1. This asana is extremely beneficial for the digestive and reproductive systems.

2. It stretches the stomach and intestines, alleviating constipation.

3. This asana loosens up the vertebrae and stimulates spinal nerves,

thus relieving backache, lumbago, rounded back and drooping shoulders.

4. Regular practice of this asana also helps make spine flexible and strengthens the lumber region. And it also helps strengthen the knees, thighs and the groin area.

5. The front of the neck is fully stretched, toning the organs in this region and regulating the thyroid gland.

Precautions

1. People with severe back ailments such as lumbago should not attempt this asana without expert guidance.

2. Those suffering from enlarged thyroid glands or goitre should also take expert guidance before doing this asana.

3. Patients with high blood pressure or any disc injury must consult doctor or a good yoga practitioner before doing this asana.

❊ KANDHARASANA (SHOULDER POSE)

Method

1. Lie down on your back on the mat with the hands placed near the body.

2. Bend the knees, placing the soles of the feet flat on the floor with the heels touching the buttocks. The feet and knees may be hip width apart.

Health and Healing Through Yoga

3. Raise the buttocks, and while supporting the back with hands, arch the back upwards.

4. Try to raise the chest and navel as high as possible.

5. Keep the feet flat on the floor.

6. In the final position, the body is supported by the head, neck, shoulders, arms and feet.

7. Stay for as long as possible and slowly come back to the ground.

8. Relax with the legs outstretched.

Benefits

1. It is a very effective asana to re-align the spine. It is also good for relieving stomach and waist pain.

2. It improves the digestion by stretching, massaging the colon and abdominal region.

3. This asana is very effective for women suffering from menstrual disorder and uterus problems.

4. It is also helpful in spermatorrhoea, prolapse, asthma, bronchial and thyroid disorders.

Precautions

1. Those suffering from duodenal ulcer, peptic ulcer or abdominal hernia should not practice kandharasana as this can cause further aggravation.

2. It is also suggested that pregnant women should avoid this asana.

Method

1. Lie flat on the stomach.

2. Raise the head and shoulders.

3. Rest the chin in the palms of the hands with the elbows on the floor.

4. Ensure to keep your elbows together so as to form a more pronounced arch to the spine.

5. Maintain a slight distance between the elbows so as to relieve excess pressure on the neck.

6. In this asana, effect is felt at two points - the neck and the lower back.

Note: Make sure that the elbows are not too far in front as this will lead to strain in the neck. Also, the elbows should not be too close to the chest as this will again cause tension in the lower back. It is therefore important to adjust the position of the elbows so that the weight is equally balanced on the two points (neck and lower back). This leads to the ideal posture of this asana wherein spine is equally relaxed.

Benefits

1. This asana is a boon for those suffering from slipped disc, sciatica, lower back pain.

2. This asana encourages the vertebral column to resume its normal shape and releases compression of the spinal nerves.

3. It is a must for those suffering from asthma and other lung ailments as this asana allows more air to enter the lungs.

Precaution

In case any severe pain is experienced while doing this asana, which could be because of pre-existing back problem, consult a yoga practitioner before pursuing the practise of this asana.

❋ SARPASANA (SNAKE POSE)

Method

1. Lie flat in prone (face down) position on the floor.

2. Rest the chin on the floor, keeping the legs straight and the feet together.

3. Stretch the toes out, with the upper feet touching the floor.

4. Interlock the fingers of both hands behind the buttocks.

5. Keep the elbows straight and lift the arms behind the back.

6. Using the lower back muscles, slowly raise the head, shoulders and chest as much as possible from the floor.

7. Push the hands further back and raise the arms as high as possible.

8. Raise the body as high as possible without straining and squeeze the shoulder blades together while looking forward.

9. Hold only for as long as is comfortable.

10. Slowly return to the starting position and relax the whole body.

11. Release the hands and relax the arms by sides of the body.

Benefits

1. The benefits of this asana are same as those of bhujangasana with an increased influence on the chest.

2. This asana pressurises the air within the lungs and helps to open out inactive alveoli, improving both the removal of carbon dioxide and the intake of oxygen.

3. Due to the increased pressure within the chest cavity, the heart is toned and strengthened.

4. Regular practise of this asana is very useful for those suffering from asthma.

5. Besides physical benefits, the persistent practise of sarpasana helps to release blocked emotions.

Precautions

1. People with heart problems and high blood pressure should take care not to strain while performing this asana.

2. In case you experience severe pain while doing this asana, please consult a good yoga instructor before practising it further.

CHAPTER 9

Pranayama

Prana means energy - this energy has not only given rise to the entire external world but has also created our gross body. The human body is composed of trillions of cells.

The nuclei present in the cells contain genes in packages called chromosomes. There are 46 chromosomes in each cell – 23 from the mother and 23 from the father. These include 22 pairs of autosomes and a pair of sex chromosomes, X and Y. In males, this includes one X and one Y, whereas females have two X chromosomes.

Each chromosome is made up of genes. Genes contain the information to make proteins, the body's building blocks. Proteins make up the structure of organs and tissues. Each protein performs a specific job in different types of cells and the information for making at least one protein is contained in a single gene.

Analysis of the ultra structure of a cell will finally lead to an atom – energy present in an atom is ordinarily beyond our comprehension. Our sages and seers called this energy as prana - the cosmic energy. As the sages delved deeper, their understanding brought them to the conclusion that this energy is responsible for the creation and maintenance of not only every living being but also all inanimate objects. The science of pranayama was developed on the basis of this fundamental principle.

Pranayama entails augmentation of the prana energy. This revelation did not exclusively happen in India but also in China. In China, the prana energy is called `chi'; the science of acupressure and acupuncture are based on this energy. As per the Chinese doctrine, there are several meridians in the human body through which this energy flows - diseases are the result of blockage in this flow. The meridians – or nadis as we call them in yoga – are not gross, physical entities; they are subtle channels along which the energy flows. It is, hence, not surprising that these meridians are not revealed by dissection of the human body.

There are five types of prana energy - apana, vyana, udana, samana, prana. The entire human body is governed by the energy of prana. There is an old vedic story about prana that we find in various Upanishads - mind, prana, and five sense organs began to argue with each other as to which one of them was the best and most important. This reflects the ordinary human state in which our faculties are not integrated but fight with each other, competing for their rule over our attention. To resolve this dispute they decided that each would leave the body and see whose absence was most missed.

First, speech left the body but the body continued, though mute. Next, eyes left but the body continued, though blind. Next, the ears left but the body continued, though deaf. Mind left but the body continued, though unconscious. Finally, the prana began to leave and the body began to die and all the other faculties began to lose their energy. So they all rushed to prana and pleaded it to stay, lauding its supremacy. Prana gives energy to all our faculties, without which they cannot function. We cannot do anything without prana energy. The moral of this story is that to have command over our other faculties, it is essential to have command over prana.

Prana operates on many levels and can be interpreted in many ways - from the breath to the energy of consciousness itself. Prana is not only the basic life force but it is the prime form of all energy, working on the level of mind and body. Indeed, the entire universe is a manifestation of prana, which is the original creative power. Even kundalini shakti, the serpent power or inner power that transforms consciousness, develops from the awakened prana.

On a cosmic level there are two basic aspects of prana. The first is the unmanifest aspect of prana, which is the energy of pure consciousness that transcends all creation. The second or manifest aspect of prana is the force of creation itself. Prana arises from the quality (guna) of rajas, the active force of nature (prakriti). Nature herself consists of three gunas: sattva or harmony, which gives rise to the mind, rajas or movement, which gives rise to the prana, and tamas or inertia that gives rise to the body.

Indeed it could be argued that prakriti or nature is primarily prana or rajas. Prakriti is Shakti, energy. According to the pull or attraction of the higher self or pure consciousness (purusha) this energy becomes sattvic. By the inertia of ignorance this energy becomes tamasic.

In relation to our physical existence, prana or vital energy is a modification of the air element, primarily the oxygen we breathe that allows us to live. Yet, as air originates in ether or space, prana arises in space and remains closely connected to it. Wherever we create space, the energy or prana arise automatically.

Types of Prana

✸ PRANA

Prana, literally means the 'forward moving air' - that moves inward and governs all activities - from eating of food, drinking of water, and inhalation of air, to the reception of sensory impressions and mental experiences. It is propulsive in nature, setting things in motion and guiding them. It provides the basic energy that drives us in life.

✸ APANA

Apana literally means the 'air that moves away'. It moves downwards and outwards, regulating the functioning of all body parts and organs situated below the umbilicus. This includes the gall bladder, liver, small and large intestines. Hence, it governs digestion of the ingested food and elimination of waste matter i.e. urine and faeces. In addition, it controls functioning of the male and female reproductive organs. On a deeper level, it rules the elimination of negative sensory, emotional and mental experiences. It is the basis of our immune function at all levels.

✳ UDANA

Udana literally means the 'upward moving air' and regulates body parts situated above the throat. This includes functioning of the eyes, ears, nose and tongue (taste and speech). It governs growth of the body, the ability to stand, speech, effort, enthusiasm and will. It is our main positive energy in life through which we can develop our different bodies and evolve in consciousness.

✳ SAMANA

Samana literally means 'balancing air' - moves from the periphery to the centre, through a churning and discerning action. It works on the middle portion of the body and maintains a balance between apana and prana. It aids in digestion on all levels - it works in the gastro-intestinal tract to digest food, in the lungs to digest air or absorb oxygen, and in the mind to homogenise and digest experiences, whether sensory, emotional or mental.

✳ VYANA

Vyana literally means the 'outward moving air' - moves from the centre to the periphery. It pervades the entire body and governs circulation on all levels. It moves the food, water and oxygen throughout the body, and keeps our emotions and thoughts circulating in the mind, imparting movement and providing strength. And in doing so it assists all the other pranas in their work.

The five pranas are energies and processes that occur on several levels. However, we can localise them in a few key ways - prana vayu governs the movement of energy from the head down to the navel, which is the pranic centre in the physical body. Apana vayu governs the movement of energy from the navel down to the root chakra. Samana vayu governs the balancing of energy from the entire body back to the navel. Vyana vayu governs the movement of energy out from the navel throughout the entire body. Udana vayu governs the movement of energy from the navel up to the head.

To sum up, we can conclude that prana governs the intake of substances, samana governs their digestion, vyana governs the circulation of nutrients, udana governs the release of positive energy, and apana governs the elimination of waste-materials.

This is similar to the working of a machine. Prana brings in the fuel, samana converts this fuel to energy, vyana circulates the energy to the various work sites, apana releases the waste materials or by products of the conversion process, and udana governs the positive energy created in the process and determines the work that the machine is able to do.

The key to health and wellbeing is to keep our pranas in harmony. When one prana becomes imbalanced, the others tend to become imbalanced as well because they are all linked together. Generally, prana and udana work opposite to apana as the forces of energisation versus those of elimination. Similarly, vyana and samana are opposites as expansion and contraction.

How Prana Creates the Physical Body

Without prana, the physical body is nothing more than a lump of clay. Prana sculpts this gelatinous mass into various limbs and organs. It does this by creating various subtle channels or nadis, through which it can operate and energise gross matter into various tissues and organs.

Prana vayu creates the openings and channels in the head and brain down to the heart. There are seven openings in the head: two eyes, two ears, two nostrils and mouth.

Udana assists prana in creating the openings in the upper part of the body, particularly those of the mouth and vocal organs. The mouth, after all, is the main opening in the head and in the entire body. It could be said that the entire physical body is an extension of the mouth, which is the main organ of physical activity, eating and self-expression.

Apana vayu creates the openings in the lower part of the body, those of the uro-genital and excretory systems.

Samana vayu creates the openings in the middle part of the body, those of the digestive system, centred in the navel. It opens out the channels of intestines and the organs like liver and pancreas.

Vyana vayu creates the channels going to the peripheral parts of the body, the arms and legs. It creates the veins and arteries, muscles, sinews, joints and bones.

Hence, samana vayu creates the trunk of the body (which is dominated by the gastro-intestinal tract), while vyana vayu creates the limbs, prana and udana create the upper openings or bodily orifices, while apana creates those below.

Prana, however, does not exist just on the physical level. The navel is the main vital centre for the physical body, the heart is the main centre for the pranamaya kosha, and the head is the main centre for manomaya kosha.

Prana and Breath

Breathing is the main form of pranic activity in the body. Prana governs inhalation, samana governs absorption of oxygen that occurs mainly during retention of the breath, vyana governs its circulation, apana governs exhalation and the release of carbon dioxide, and udana governs exhalation and the release of positive energy through breath, including speech that occurs via the outgoing breath.

Prana and Mind

The mind too has its energy and prana which it derives from food, breath and impressions. Prana governs the intake of sensory impressions, samana governs mental assimilation, vyana governs mental dissemination, apana governs the elimination of toxic ideas and negative emotions, and udana governs positive mental energy, strength and enthusiasm.

On the psychological level, prana governs our receptivity to positive sources of nourishment, feelings and knowledge through the mind and senses. When deranged, it leads to perverse desires and insatiable craving - we become misguided, misdirected and generally out of balance.

Koshas

Kosha means a sheath and the human body consists of five koshas: annamaya (physical body), pranamaya (cosmic energy), manomaya (mind), vigyanamaya (intellect or ego) and anandamaya (causal blissful body). Annamaya kosha refers to our body. The kosha that is born of the anna (grain), is nurtured by the anna, is sustained by the anna and finally merges with the anna, is called the annamaya kosha. After the annamaya kosha is pranamaya kosha which I am going to explain in detail later. Manomaya kosha is the third sheath. And to put it simply, the mind is the manomaya kosha, including sensory impressions. Sub-conscious, conscious and unconscious are the three major levels of the mind in the manomaya kosha. After this is the fourth one, vigyanamaya kosha. Vigyanamaya kosha has the aspects of intellect and ahankara associated with it. And the fifth sheath is anandamaya kosha, the dimension of bliss, wholeness, contentment and superconscious mind.

❋ PRANAMAYA KOSHA

The pranamaya kosha is the sphere of our vital life energies. This sheath mediates between the body on one side and the three sheaths of the mind (outer mind, intelligence and inner mind) on the other and acts on both levels. It mediates between the five gross elements and the five sensory impressions.

Pranamaya kosha consists of our vital urges of survival, reproduction, movement and self-expression, being mainly connected to the five motor organs (excretory, uro-genital, feet, hands, and tongue).

The vital body and its deep-seated urges, that are necessary for us to remain alive, dominate lives of most of the people. This is also where the subconscious ego dwells - which holds the various fears, desires and attachments. We spend most of our time seeking enjoyment in the form of sensory pleasure and acquisition of material objects.

A person with a strong dynamic nature becomes prominent in life and is able to impress his personality upon the world. Those with a weak dull disposition lack the power to accomplish anything and usually remain in a subordinate position. Generally people who are aggressive and have an egotistic proclivity run the world, while those with weak predisposition follow them - such a tenacious, egocentric predilection is one of the greatest obstacles to the spiritual path.

A strong pranamaya kosha is important for the spiritual path, but this is very different from the egotistic or desire oriented vital. It derives its strength not from our personal power but by surrendering to the divine and its exalted energy. Without a strong spiritual vital, we lack the power to do our spiritual practices.

Secret to Mastery over the Pranas

Pranayama is not only related to breath and its regulation, but it is directly concerned with the five pranas present in the body. If you gain full control and mastery over the pranas, then anything is possible. Yogis have demonstrated that heart, pulse, blood circulation too can be stopped. Actions of the brain, heart and sense organs are controlled by udana vayu – its area of work can be understood through the practice of pranayama. Scores of yogis have gained mastery on the body and mind - I have personally met some, including Swami Rama and Swami Bua; but there are many more living anonymously.

There are several different types of pranayama. Some are practiced to increase the heat in the body and some to cool it down, while some are practiced to achieve equilibrium in breathing and brain activity.

As per Patanjali's eightfold path - a strong base of yama, niyama, asana and pranayama (outward/external means and methods) is essential before moving inward.

Yama means 'restraint' or moral code of conduct while interacting with others. They are: satya – truthfulness; ahimsa - non-violence; asteya - non-stealing; brahmacharya – chastity; aparigraha - non-hoarding.

The second limb of Patanjali's eightfold path continues to harness the energy the regular practice of moral discipline. Niyama is self-restraint, forming a strong base for spiritual growth. They are: shaucha – purity and cleanliness; santosha – contentment; tapas – austerity; swadhyaya - self-study of scriptures; ishwara pranidhana - surrendering to God's will.

Without the practice of yama and niyama, just doing asanas will not lead to any deeper benefit. These days many people do asanas only to restore physical health and beauty.

It's only when yama, niyama, asanas and pranayama are perfected that one can move inwards to practice the internal steps of yoga – pratyahara (withdrawing the mind from the sense organs), dharana, dhyana and samadhi. Hence, path of yoga is an eight-fold path. It is a hierarchal process i.e. once you have leapt from first step, one moves towards the second and thereafter cross all the other steps. Pranayama can be mastered only after asanas have been honed; dharana can be achieved only when pranayama has been perfected and dhyana is the fruition of dharana. Samadhi is the ultimate culmination of matured dhyana. A firm resolve, patience and determination are paramount on this arduous path as the process is gradual - there are no short cuts.

In the absence of self-discipline, austerity, introspection and devotion to Guru, self-realisation and samadhi cannot be achieved. It is not possible to achieve anything on this path without grace and guidance from the Guru; devotion to God is inclusive of devotion to Guru.

If you practice asana while observing yama and niyama, then the asanas will also have an effect on the annamaya, manomaya and pranamaya koshas.

Ida, Pingala and Sushumna

Our mood is controlled by chemical secretions produced by the endocrine glands. When you are angry, it is not 'you' who is angry; it is a manifestation of bodily impurity, or rather of mental impurity. This also indicates that ida and pingala nadis are not in balance and sushumna is not yet awakened thereby propelling the person in the whirlpool of emotions and moods.

The three major nadis (subtle energy channels) are: ida, pingala and sushumna. When the breath moves through the left nostril, it is not just the breath alone – it is ida which is active, and when it moves through the right nostril it is pingala which is active. The interchange between the flow of ida and pingala happens every eighty to ninety minutes. If ida flows more than pingala, there will be an adverse effect on brain and mind. So to maintain a balance between their flow, asanas and pranayama are quintessential.

The person whose ida nadi is awakened is mentally active, dynamic, creative, reflective and receptive - all scientists have an active and awakened ida. But the activation of ida is not as simple as closing right nostril and breathing from the left. This leads to the question - what does activation of ida and pingala really entail?

Nadi does not mean a nerve; it is a subtle energy channel, a flow that starts at the muladhara chakra and ends at the ajña chakra. The third nadi – the sushumna – also reaches the ajña chakra, hence this chakra is also symbolically referred to as Prayaga (confluence point of the three rivers Ganga, Yamuna and Saraswati). In yogic science, pingala is called as Ganga, ida as Yamuna and sushumna as Saraswati.

Hence, ajña chakra is the symbolic internal Prayaga reflecting the external confluence of the three rivers at Prayaga - an important Hindu pilgrimage. In the outside world too, the Saraswati is not visible; Hindus believe that it is hidden and invisible, but it is certain that this river flows. The confluence of the rivers – Ganga, Yamuna and Saraswati – is known as Prayaga or the meeting point. Prayaga is considered a famous and an important pilgrimage for Hindus. This, however, is the external Prayaga, but for a yogi - the ajña chakra is the internal and true Prayaga.

When pingala is awakened, the person is active, industrious and perseverant. Such people work without any concern for the fruit of their actions. They do not strive for personal gain; if they earn money, it is with a view to benefit society and the country. And they become efficient politicians, statesmen, army generals and soldiers. Nature creates opportunities for progress and advancement for those whose pingala is awakened.

If neither the ida nor the pingala are awakened, a person will not progress in life; he will not be active or reflective. His life will be limited to indulgence in the sense organs i.e. eating, drinking and being hedonistic.

This also implies that if an aspirant makes a concerted effort, he can awaken his ida and pingala and acquire the qualities he does not possess. If the ida is awakened, the brain function improves, the person becomes contemplative and reflective, and can achieve all goals in life.

Activating Ida, Pingala and Sushumna

If you practice yama, niyama, asana and pranayama regularly, for at least one year, ida and pingala will begin to function normally - having an overall beneficial effect on the body and mind. If you faithfully cleanse your body with neti, varisara dhauti (shankha prakshalana) and vaman dhauti (kunjal kriya) for a period of 6 months to a year, you will definitely experience a progressive, positive change in your life.

Only if the ida and pingala are awakened, there arises a possibility of the awakening of the sushumna nadi. And it's only after these three nadis are awakened, that a person can begin to work on activating the chakras, have a quest for truth and awaken the kundalini. The first experience of savikalpa samadhi happens when the kundalini rises and pierces through the muladhara, manipuraka, anahata, vishuddha and ajña chakras to reach the sahasrara.

Key to Spiritual Upliftment

If you aspire for spiritual upliftment and freedom from bondage, you must understand that gyana or true knowledge cannot be obtained from listening to experiences narrated by enlightened masters or by reading the scriptures. It will only give momentary pleasure and be of no other help to you. People listen to spiritual discourses for years, but their lives remain unchanged - they fail to fathom the deep meaning inherent in the heard words.

Gyana flowers only when one possesses wisdom of discrimination, intense dispassion, detachment, keeps the company of sages and mystics. People who lack these qualities only end up with bloated egos - deluded that they are very knowledgeable as they listen to spiritual discourses.

Usually, people take shallow breaths which are just confined to the chest. There is hardly any movement of the abdomen. One needs to learn the correct breathing technique - yogic breathing. The practical method to check your breathing pattern is to observe your breath – are you doing thoracic breathing or abdominal breathing? Often it is thoracic breathing – chest rises and falls but not the stomach.

Types of Breathing

Before learning pranayama, one needs to understand the breathing process. We can breathe in three ways:

❋ ABDOMINAL BREATHING

This involves deep inhalation with breath expanding the abdomen. There is a horizontal layer of muscle right below the lungs, known as the diaphragm. When you take a long and deep breath, it causes movement of the diaphragm - pressing it downwards exerting pressure on the abdominal cavity with resultant outward movement of the anterior abdominal wall; this is known as abdominal breathing. The lungs get maximally filled up, bringing maximum prana energy to the body.

❋ SHALLOW BREATHING

The normal breath ought to reach up to the stomach, but modern man's lifestyle is such that the breath reaches only up to the chest. In this type of breathing, only half a litre of air is inhaled, which is one eighth of the total capacity of the lungs - normal lungs have the capacity to hold around four litres of air. Due to shallow breathing, the body receives much less prana energy than it should.

❋ BREATHING AT THE THROAT

If the lungs are weak or diseased, the breath is extremely short and shallow; the lungs are unable to hold even half a litre of air. This is 'breathing at the throat'.

❋ YOGIC BREATHING

The correct way of breathing is yogic breathing. All these three types of breathings happen simultaneously in yogic breathing. Our endeavour should be to make yogic breathing our normal style of breathing. And to achieve this, it is essential to practice it for at least thirty minutes, every day, systematically. While doing pranayama, remember that the breathing should always be deep and slow.

The foremost important step in yogic breathing is to ensure that the spine is erect and there is no slouching. Please bear in mind that because your breath has been short and shallow for so long, it will not become deep in just one day – this will happen slowly over a period of time, be patient!

Usually the inhaled breath is so short and shallow that it does not reach even fifty percent of the lungs. If you wish to correct the breathing pattern then start breathing by keeping your right hand on your stomach; initially keep your eyes open. When you breathe in slow and deep, the abdominal wall (for ease, I will refer to this as stomach) will automatically expand outward naturally - this cannot be forced. This process - where you take such a deep breath that the stomach expands outward is just one part of yogic breathing.

The second part of yogic breathing: after the stomach expands, and you continue to inhale, there is an extra expansion in the chest region too. How does this happen? When you take a very deep breath, you will feel your armpits and chest expand against your arms. Practice it now. Take a deep breath – watch the stomach expand. Then take your awareness to the armpits, while continuing to inhale. You will be able to feel the expansion in your lungs making your chest expand even more. Now the breath is in the middle and lower part of the lungs but not yet in the upper parts.

The third part: continue to inhale and let the chest expand more until your shoulders rise – don't raise the shoulders, it will happen automatically - it is a sign that oxygen has reached the upper parts of the lungs.

To summarise, the sequence of yogic breathing is as follows: first the stomach expands, then the chest and finally with continued inhalation, the shoulders get raised. To ensure the lungs have expanded fully, be aware of the armpits and check whether the chest has expanded fully or not.

To ensure the upper parts of the lungs have received oxygen, check whether the shoulders are slightly raised. Then, repeat this process with your eyes closed and keeping your total awareness on the breath. Keep the spine erect so that there is ample room for all parts to expand

Health and Healing Through Yoga

without restriction. With eyes shut, take a deep breath. The stomach expands, the lungs expand, and with a little extra effort – not forcefully – the shoulders are raised.

Remember that you breathe in slowly and then breathe out slowly. While inhaling, first concentrate on the stomach – its expansion and be aware of the breath going deep in. Then concentrate on the chest – when it expands, make an effort to inhale more deeply. And as the shoulders rise, yogic breathing is complete.

A piece of important advice – your breathing should not be audible. With every subsequent intake of breath, try to make the breath go even deeper and watch it as you inhale. Simultaneously also watch the parts of the body being affected by inhalation – stomach, chest, armpits, shoulders. Similarly, observe the outgoing breath.

During the entire process, the body should be kept steady. Movement of the hands, feet, shoulders or fingers are an unnecessary distraction. Sit as still as a mountain, with no stress on the face or crease on the forehead, muscles completely relaxed.

Keep your attention on the navel or on the nostrils. Do not struggle with the technique - inhale as deeply as you can without discomfort. The entire attention should be on the nostrils, the navel, or on any part in between where the breath is moving.

Another point to note – while breathing in, at some stage you will feel that you can't inhale any more – it is likely that even at that stage, the breath has not reached the upper parts of the lungs. Hence, there is a need for an extra effort to breathe in some more. When you finally reach the stage where you can't inhale anymore, then, you start breathing out very slowly and gently. When you exhale, the raised shoulders fall to their original position and the stomach contracts.

An important word of caution - at no point should the breathing be laboured, do not struggle. Your capacity for deep breathing will increase only gradually - don't try to walk all thousand miles in one day, it is futile! Mastery over the technique is not possible in a day. It is impossible. Ancient yogic scriptures say – "prana is like a lion and we need to master it slowly and steadily."

Whilst practicing yogic breathing, do not recite any mantra or imagine your Guru or revered deity. Although for a beginner it may help but finally all props have to be dropped. If thoughts arise while watching the breath, do not worry; thoughts are fleeting clouds, they will disperse. If you pay no attention to the thoughts they will disappear on their own; your concentration should be focused on being a witness of the breath. Yogic breathing technique not only makes the body healthy but also improves the concentration.

Preparation for Pranayama

Before proceeding to the pranayama techniques, certain preparations are essential - mastery of yogasanas and the resultant energy gained, along with discipline and firm resolve. It is important to bear in mind that if not practiced correctly, pranayama can cause serious harm.

Before entering the bodily temple, the yogi takes great pains to maintain purity and cleanliness. Prior to starting the practice of pranayama, ensure that the bladder and bowels are empty. Besides, the stomach should also be empty.

One can practice Pranayama four hours after a meal - although the best time is just before sunrise. Nevertheless, pranayama done before lunch and at sunset is also of special benefit. Other than people who have devoted their lives to yogasadhana, everyone should keep aside at least half an hour a day for practicing pranayama. March and September are good months to start the practice as the climate is rather equitable.

A clean, calm, quiet and well-ventilated room, free of insects should be used for pranayama. Do not do pranayama when you are otherwise busy. Practice with regularity and determination, without changing the place, time or the position of the body. The only change allowed is in the technique – for example one day you practice surya bhedana pranayama; the next day, sheetali pranayama; bhastrika on the third day and so on. However, nadi shodhana pranayama should be practiced daily.

Except for sheetali and sheetkari pranayama, in all the others, the breath must be inhaled and exhaled through the nostrils. Sit on a rug. The asanas recommended for practicing pranayama are: siddhasana, siddha-yoni asana, veerasana, padmasana. The spine should be erect – right from the base to the neck. Some pranayama techniques can be practiced lying down.

The muscles of the face, neck, eyes, shoulders, hands and legs should be relaxed. In particular, ensure that the hands and legs are free of tension. The tongue should be loose and motionless so that saliva does not collect in the mouth; if it does, swallow it before the inhalation.

In yoga, inhalation is called puraka, exhalation is called rechaka and retention of breath is called kumbhaka. In the practice of pranayama, the aspirant should not attempt to exceed the limits of his capacity. For example, if you practice 10 second rechaka and 10 second puraka for five minutes with some discomfort, then stop at seven or eight seconds when there is no discomfort. Do not stress the lungs further - do not fall short of breath while practicing. Never try to exceed your limits - slowly the capacity to inhale and exhale deeper can be achieved. Remember, incorrectly done pranayama shakes the very foundation of the mind and body. The inhaled and exhaled breath should be balanced. If it is difficult to maintain the rhythm of steady, deep and long breathing, then you must discontinue the practice.

Pranayama should be done after performing yogasana, but not immediately after difficult asanas – the body being tired, the spine may not stay erect. After asanas, always take a rest in shavasana for minimum of fifteen minutes, then sit with your spine erect and begin pranayama.

Nadi shodhana and ujjayi pranayama, when done whilst sitting in baddhakonasana, is extremely beneficial for expectant mothers. In the absence of an experienced teacher, you may use a good book which can explain how to sit in baddhakonasana, but one thing which is to be remembered is that a pregnant woman must not do kumbhaka - retention of breath.

Initially one may sweat or shiver, but these symptoms will disappear with regular practice. The eyes should be kept closed right through the practice or else the practice will be bereft of concentration.

Regular and continuous practice of pranayama changes a person's mindset. Sensual desires like food craving, smoking, drinking and sexual urges, are greatly reduced. Focus of the sense organs is turned inwards and the aspirant starts becoming introspective; ability to hear the internal sounds of silence is enhanced – thus pranayama lays the foundation for pratyahara and dissolves the dominance of the senses over the mind.

There are several techniques of pranayama. Following are the seven key techniques:

❋ Nadi Shodhana Pranayama

Right through this pranayama, the hands are held in the nasagra mudra. Bring the right hand in front of the face (if it gets tired, the left hand can be used). Place the tips of the middle and index fingers on the point between the eyebrows. Place the thumb near the right nostril and the ring and small finger near the left nostril. The thumb and ring finger will be used alternately to open and close the right and left nostril respectively, as required. Place the right elbow in front, touching the chest. This is nasagra mudra.

First Stage

Sit in a comfortable asana. Keep the spine erect, but without undue stress. The body should be in such a comfortable position, that the need to move due to any sort of discomfort does not arise for at least 15 minutes. Place the left hand on the left knee or in the lap. Close the right nostril with the right thumb and slowly inhale and exhale through the left nostril; the breath should be slow, deep and stress-free. Be aware of the breath at all times. After five minutes, open the right nostril, close the left nostril with the ring finger and repeat the same procedure. When you obtain mastery over this technique and are able to do it easily and without stress, proceed to the next technique.

The second technique is essentially similar to the first but the duration of the breath is controlled. No undue stress should be exerted while breathing. Take a deep breath for a count of three; exhale to a count of six - the exhalation should be twice as long as the inhalation. Do 10 rounds of this process, first through the left nostril and then 10 rounds through the right nostril. One inhalation and one exhalation constitute one round. If time permits, this technique can be practiced for a longer period without any ill effects.

Second Stage

Sit steady and form the nasagra mudra (as described above) with the right hand. Close the right nostril and take a slow and deep breath from the left nostril. While breathing in, expand the stomach and chest, taking in as much air into the lungs as possible. Breathe easy without any stress. Now close the left nostril and open the right, slowly exhaling – the slower the better. Empty the lungs completely. Then, inhale slowly and deeply through the right nostril. When the lungs are filled to capacity, close the right nostril, open the left and slowly exhale. This is one cycle of nadi shodhana pranayama.

Be continuously aware of the breath and do ten to fifteen rounds everyday - begin with fewer rounds and keep on adding more rounds every day. Practice this technique with regularity and gain expertise in it as per your ability.

Keeping a gap of one second between two counts, attempt to gain control over the duration of rechaka and puraka; the count for both should be the same. After a few weeks of practice, try to increase the duration of rechaka and puraka, keeping them equal.

Third Stage

In the third stage, one needs to be totally aware of both, the count and the breath. This stage is essentially similar to the second stage – difference is that in this stage one has to maintain the duration of puraka while increase the duration of rechaka. For example, if puraka is done for a count of five, then rechaka should be done for a count of six. When you become proficient in this, then while keeping the puraka count at five, increase the rechaka count to seven. Slowly, increase this to a ratio of 1:2 - puraka for a count of five and rechaka for a count of 10.

After reaching this stage, go on slowly increasing the duration of puraka, and correspondingly of rechaka - this may take several months. In this way, with regular practice, increase your capacity slowly and gain mastery over the technique of a slow and long puraka, and an ever slower and longer rechaka.

There are several other advanced techniques of nadi shodhana, but these should be practiced only under the supervision of an experienced teacher. For beginners, the techniques listed above should suffice.

The persistent practise of nadi shodhana yields great benefits. It nourishes the whole body by an extra supply of oxygen; carbon dioxide is efficiently expelled and the blood is purified of toxins. It also stimulates the brain centres ensuing their optimum functioning, induces tranquillity, clarity of thought and concentration, and is highly recommended for those engaged in mental work. It increases vitality and lowers levels of stress and anxiety by harmonising the pranas. It clears pranic blockages and balances ida and pingala nadis, causing sushumna nadi to flow, which leads to deep states of meditation and spiritual awakening.

❋ UJJAYI PRANAYAMA

Sit in an appropriate posture – padmasana, veerasana, siddhasana or sahajasana. Place the hands on the knees forming the gyana mudra or chin mudra - back erect, spine should be erect.

Close your eyes, delve inwards and bring the awareness to the region of the throat, perceiving the passing breath. While gently constricting the throat, take steady, slow and deep breaths from both nostrils. The inhaled breath will touch the palate and the upper part of the throat and a gentle hissing sound will become discernable. This process of inhalation is called puraka.

Make sure that the inhaled breath completely fills the lungs with air; hold it in for a second or two. Holding the breath in is called antarkumbhaka. Exhale slowly, gently and deeply, emptying the lungs completely. The exhaled breath will touch the palate and the upper part of the throat - there will be a gentle humming sound like `hmmm'. This process of exhalation is called rechaka. Hold the breath at this stage for two seconds before starting with puraka again.

This completes one cycle of ujjayi pranayama. As per the individual's capacity, this should be done for 5 to 10 minutes. Ujjayi pranayama can be done in the day or night, while walking or lying down - there is no limitation on the number of cycles.

Ujjayi strengthens the lungs and eradicates the problem of phlegm. It also balances the lymphatic system. Ujjayi pranayama done while lying down - but without kumbhaka - is greatly beneficial to patients of high blood pressure, insomnia and strengthens the nervous system.

✳ SURYA BHEDANA PRANAYAMA

In this pranayama, the breath is taken in through the right nostril i.e. the pingala nadi - also known as the solar nadi. Then the breath is held in (antarkumbhaka) for some time and finally exhaled from the left nostril, the ida nadi - also known as the lunar nadi.

Sit in an appropriate asana keeping the spine erect. Keep the left wrist on the left knee and form the nasagra mudra with the right hand. Close the left nostril with the ring finger of the right hand. Holding the thumb of the right hand in the proximity of the right nostril, take a deep breath and fill the lungs to capacity with air. Now close the right nostril also both the nostrils are now closed – hold the breath in. There should be no stress or strain. Keeping the right nostril closed, breathe out very slowly through the half opened left nostril.

This completes one cycle of the surya bhedana pranayama; practice it according to your ability for 5 to 10 minutes.

In this pranayama, puraka is done through the right nostril and rechaka through the left. While doing this pranayama, pay attention to and be fully aware of the places where the incoming and outgoing breath touches. The eyes, ears, forehead and eyebrows should be totally immobile but without any stress. Puraka and rechaka should be of equal duration.

This pranayama improves the digestion. The lymphatic system is refreshed and relaxed and the nasal pathway is cleansed. Patients with low blood pressure are especially benefitted by this pranayama. However, it is important to note that people suffering from high blood pressure and heart disease should never - in the practice of any pranayama - do antarkumbhaka i.e. holding the breath in.

The word bhastrika means bellows. As the ironmonger's bellows fan the fire, in the same way, the breath is rapidly inhaled and exhaled.

First Stage

Sit in padmasana, siddhasana, veerasana or sahajasana. Place the left hand on the left knee in gyana mudra or chin mudra. Keep the spine erect, close the eyes and concentrate the mind inwards. With the right hand, form the nasagra mudra.

Empty the lungs completely. Close the right nostril with the right hand thumb. Then, breathe forcefully and vigorously through the left nostril. Fill the lungs completely with air and then exhale – again - forcefully and vigorously.

Be aware, that with the breathing, only the abdomen expands and retracts – the chest should not move. The vigorous breathing leads to a sound resembling air rushing through bellows. The inhalation and exhalation should be rhythmic. One inhalation and one exhalation completes one cycle. Practice 10 to 12 cycles through the left nostril.

Second Stage

Repeat the entire process through the right nostril, after closing the left nostril.

Third Stage

Repeat the above process simultaneously through both the nostrils.

Completion of the third stage equals to one cycle. Beginners should start with five cycles of this pranayama. As the stomach muscles become strengthened with regular practice, the number of cycles and the duration of antarkumbhaka can be increased slowly to one minute. Although any number of cycles of bhastrika can be done with no ill effect, 10 rounds are sufficient.

Note of caution: If while doing the practice, you experience any sweating, tremor or nausea, then the practice should be discontinued immediately. Bhastrika pranayama is not advisable for the patients suffering from high blood pressure, heart disease or hernia.

There are several benefits of bhastrika: it brings about amazing improvements in the entire lifestyle, filling the mind with peace and joy; it removes all physical problems; it removes tridosha; it speeds up the flow of prana energy in the body; it improves the functioning of the entire nervous system.

❋ KAPALABHATI PRANAYAMA

In bhastrika pranayama, both puraka and rechaka are done rapidly with force, whereas in kapalabhati pranayama, puraka is done slowly and effortlessly and rechaka is done forcefully. The difference is that inhalation is passive but exhalation is active and vigorous. The exhaled breath will contract the stomach muscles and force the air out of the lungs. In this entire procedure, the breath is controlled from the stomach and the chest is not expanded or contracted.

Sit in any comfortable pranayama posture, keeping the spine erect. Close the eyes and take the awareness inwards.

Take a quick breath from the stomach, then, contracting the stomach muscles breathe out forcefully. Slowly, without effort, let the stomach muscles expand. Do not make an attempt to inhale - just breathe in as much that happens without any effort.

Keep a gentle pause in between the inhalations and exhalations, repeating this technique with speed for some time. Then, take in a deep and slow breath. Now do rechaka and empty the lungs completely - do the mula bandha. This completes one cycle of kapalabhati pranayama.

If no fatigue is experienced, then start the second cycle. Beginners should take only 20 quick breaths i.e. two cycles of 10 to 12 breaths. Gradually increase the number of breaths till you are able to do 60 to 100 breaths per cycle.

This pranayama is not recommended for patients suffering from high blood pressure, heart disease and hernia. Its benefits are similar to those of bhastrika – it improves awareness, cleanses and strengthens the lungs.

Sit in any asana appropriate for pranayama and relax the body. Open the mouth and form an 'O' with the lips. Roll the tongue in the form of a tube, so that the sides touch each other – this resembles a hollow tube, through which one will breathe. The tip of the tongue, just about protrudes through the half opened lips. Slowly take a deep breath through the rolled up tongue; draw in the air past the rolled tongue with a sibilant sound (sssss) to fill the lungs completely. Draw the tongue in and close the mouth.

Press the chin to the chest and do the jalandhar bandha, holding in the breath for some time.

Then raise the head and breathe out through the nose. This is one cycle - do as many cycles as you can do comfortably.

As the name of this pranayama suggests, the practice of this pranayama cools the body system. It improves digestion and relieves thirst.

✽ SHEETKARI PRANAYAMA

Health and Healing Through Yoga

In this pranayama, the tongue is not to be rolled, just part the lips and gently clench the teeth. Breathe in through the gap between the upper and lower teeth. Take a long deep breath and after doing puraka, turn the tongue backwards in the mouth such that the lower part of the tongue touches the palate.

Holding in the breath for some time, do the jalandhar bandha. Then raise the head and release the bandha. Slowly breathe out through both nostrils. This completes one cycle of sheetkari pranayama. You can do as many as required and convenient. It is advisable that you learn the method of jalandhar bandha from a Sadguru.

In both sheetali and sheetkari pranayama, the air is breathed in through the mouth, so it reaches the lungs directly without being filtered. Since the microbes present in the air reach the lungs, therefore it is very important that these pranayama are not done in an unclean environment. The various asanas and pranayama techniques raise the body heat - to balance it and cool the body, these two methods of pranayama are very beneficial.

CHAPTER 10

Shatkarma

Hatha yoga is a crucial part of Yoga. However, it is wrong to assume that its realm is limited only to physical aspects of the body, for the reason that it also deals with internal cleansing of the body. Hatha yoga is not about asana and pranayama alone - it plays a significant role in evolution of human consciousness. For a spiritual aspirant, hatha yoga is of paramount importance for progressing on the spiritual path as it leads to wisdom and spiritual effulgence.

This entire creation is permeated with the two opposite polarities – negative and positive. These two polarities are also present in the human body - existing as ida nadi and as pingala nadi. The primary objective of hatha yoga is to balance the flow of these two types of energies. As a result, flow of prana energy begins in the sushumna nadi, located in between ida and pingala, which ascends the seeker to the heights of spiritual evolution.

Ida, pingala and sushumna exist in the subtle body and not in the physical or gross body. Hence, if one dissects the human body, there will be no trace of these subtle energy channels – the sanskrit word nadi means 'flow of energy' and not 'nerve' as it is mistakenly understood. It is very important that one understands these energy channels – as one gains mastery on the energy flow in these channels, it will stimulate the seeker to scale greater heights on the spiritual path. All the branches of yoga aim to evolve human consciousness and the techniques of hatha yoga are unprecedented in this context.

Shatkarma

An impure body is not fit to do sadhana. Hence, a spiritual seeker needs to cleanse the body of all unwanted elements - phlegm, trapped air and faeces etc. need to be eliminated from the body. The first requirement of the aspirant on the spiritual path is cleansing of the gross body, without which advanced yogic practices are not possible. To achieve this, our ancient yogis defined six methods in hatha yoga – these are known as shatkarma, namely

NETI - Nasal cleansing
DHAUTI - Cleansing of the digestive tract
NAULI - Abdominal massage
BASTI - Colon cleansing
KAPALABHATI - Purification and vitalisation of the frontal lobes
TRATAKA - Fixed gazing without blinking

The ancient yogis of India have explained yogic practices in a scientific manner. These practices detoxify and cleanse the body and mind, and they also help in spiritual evolution. On the spiritual path, physical cleanliness is as important as mental purity - in fact it is of prime importance, because in the presence of physical impurities, the energies lying latent in the body and mind cannot be awakened. To this effect, yoga prescribes asana and pranayama along with hatha yoga practices like shatkarma.

❋ NETI - NASAL CLEANSING

Neti is of two types: jala or water neti and sutra or string neti. The purpose of neti is to cleanse the olfactory region - it eliminates the accumulated mucus and unwanted elements such as microbes, bacteria and other particles. It clears up the sinuses and keeps the turbinates clear.

Jala Neti

In this technique, lukewarm salt water is poured into one nostril, so that it leaves through the other. The procedure is then repeated from the nostril on the other side; the nose is then dried by bending forward and by rapid breathing.

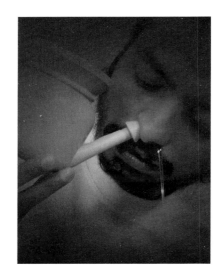

Preparation for Jala Neti

1. Neti pot specially designed for this process.

2. Tepid saline water prepared by adding 1 teaspoon of salt to every 500 ml of tepid water – the water temperature should be lukewarm, compatible with the body temperature and should be easily tolerated in the nostrils.

Method

1. Fill the neti pot with the tepid saline water, as described above.

2. Turn the head slowly to the right and place the spout of the pot in the left nostril. Tilt the pot such that the water flows into the left nostril.

3. Keep the mouth open right through the entire process, breathing only from the mouth.

4. Tilt the head down slowly towards right, so that the water flows through the back of the left nostril into the right side and exits from the right nostril. If the position of the head and pot is correct, and if the breathing is done through the mouth, the procedure will take place naturally without any effort.

5. Let the water flow out freely through the right nostril for

about 20 seconds.

6. Now remove the pot.

7. It is very important that there is no residual water remaining in the nostrils. To ensure this, breathe forcefully as in kapalabhati pranayama to expel all the water. The exhaled breath should not be too forceful as that can cause damage.

8. Repeat the entire process with the right nostril. Place the spout of the neti pot in the right nostril and tilt the head to the left. The water will enter the left nostril through the back of the right nostril; let the water flow out freely through the left nostril. Repeat the rest of the procedure, steps 6 and 7, as stated above.

Drying the Nostrils

If the residual water is not expelled from the nostrils and sinuses, it can prove to be harmful - therefore, using the following technique, clear out all the water.

1. Stand with both the feet together and fold the hands behind the back.

2. Bend down from the waist with the head raised up, holding the pose for 30 seconds; all the water will drain out. Continue to hold the position and breathe forcefully through the nose 5 to 10 times.

3. Now stand straight.

4. Close one nostril and breathe rapidly through the other 30 times. Concentrate on exhaling forcefully so that all the water is expelled.

5. Now repeat the same process with the other nostril, ensuring all the water is expelled.

6. Now repeat the process with both the nostrils open.

7. Sit in shashankasana for some time with head down and hips on the heels; remain in this pose for some time and then do kapalabhati for 20 to 30 times.

After following this simple technique, there will not be even a drop of water left in the nostrils. In case you feel that some water is still remaining in the nostrils, you can continue to follow this technique until all the water is cleared and the nostrils are dry.

Special Note

People with an obstruction in the nasal passage will be unable to follow this technique successfully - they should instead, practice sutra or string neti. Initially, the eyes may appear bloodshot but this condition will disappear in a few days. Neti can be practiced every morning even during winters. This process is not unnatural - our eyes secrete tears from the tear ducts to clear the eyes. In neti, we use the same technique i.e. the tepid saline water (similar to tears) which clears up bacteria or microbes trapped in mucus lining.

Benefits

The practice of jala neti eradicates all impurities from the nose and the sinuses. It helps in curing the common cold. Its regular practice alleviates several diseases of the ears, nose, eyes and throat – for example, some types of hearing defects, weak eyesight, enlargement of the Adam's apple and enlarged adenoids. If you ever suffer from a headache - avoid taking a tablet. Just pick up your neti pot and do jala neti!

Besides being beneficial for the body, the technique of jala neti has a profound positive effect on the mind as well. It has a beneficial effect on epilepsy, acute headaches, uncontrolled temper, etc. – both the mind and body are refreshed, removing lassitude and lethargy.

Spiritual Benefits

1. Jala neti stimulates the paranasal sinuses and assists in the awakening of the ajña chakra. All nadis from the nose to the brain are affected by

this procedure; it removes all blockages in the area of the brain helping the flow of energy to be normalised.

2. Jala neti has a beneficial effect on the frontal lobes and other parts of the brain - this may also lead to the awakening of extra-sensory perceptions. It enhances concentration and memory, facilitating meditation on the ajña chakra.

Precautions

1. It is recommended that in the beginning, this technique should be followed under the guidance of a trained yoga teacher. The water should flow only through the nose – if it flows from the throat or mouth, it means that the angle of the head is not correct. You must correct the angle, so that water flows only from the nose. After jala neti, the nostrils should be completely dried out or else you may begin to experience a sensation in the nostrils which may resemble the symptoms of a common cold.

2. The objective of jala neti is to cleanse the nasal region and make it healthy. Therefore, do not do rechaka kriya (blowing nostril/s to drain water residue) too forcefully as it may damage the nostrils. If you suffer from chronic nasal bleeding, do not attempt this kriya without the guidance of a yoga teacher.

✳ VARISARA DHAUTI (SHANKHA PRAKSHALANA)

Varisara Dhauti (shankha prakshalana) is a part of the dhauti cleansing technique – which is concerned with cleansing of the entire gastro-intestinal tract from the mouth to the anus. The word prakshalana means complete cleaning and this is an important yet simple technique in hatha yoga.

Varisara Dhauti can be further subdivided into laghoo shankha prakshalana, a short form in which only six glasses of warm saline water are taken and expelled, and poorna shankha prakshalana, the full form in which sixteen glasses are taken and expelled.

Laghoo Shankha Prakshalana

Laghoo shankha prakshalana cleanses the small and large intestines, which are 32 feet long, present in the abdomen. Undigested food adheres to the walls of the intestines in the form of faecal matter - this makes a person irritable and short tempered. If you ever see an angry and irritable person, know that his intestines need cleansing. Laghoo shankha prakshalana cleanses all parts of the lower intestinal tract, leading to the release of energy.

Method

(a). Do not eat anything heavy a day before doing the laghoo shankha prakshalana. The stomach should be empty before the procedure – a light dinner of soup may be taken.

(b). Take a large clean utensil and fill it with six glasses of lukewarm water. Dissolve one teaspoon of salt for every half litre of water.

(c). Wear loose clothing that is comfortable for exercise. It is recommended to do this practice in an open and stress free environment. You should not have any mental tension or worry.

(d). Drink 2 glasses of water and then do the following 5 asanas:
• Tadasana (The Heavenly Stretch Pose)
• Tiryaka Tadasana (Side Bending Stretch Pose)
• Kati Chakrasana (Waist Rotating Pose)
• Tiryaka Bhujangasana (Twisting Cobra)
• Udarakarshanasana (The Abdominal Massage Pose)

Tadasana (The Heavenly Stretch Pose)

Method

1. Stand with your feet together. Raise the arms over the head and interlock the fingers with the palms facing upwards.

2. Inhale as you stretch and straighten the arms up over your head and slowly rise up on your toes, stretching and lengthening the abdominal area.

3. Hold the breath in, whilst up in the tip toe stretch, for just a few seconds - then exhale as you slowly come down again, resting the hands on the top of your head between rounds.

4. Repeat step (2) and (3) 7 times more on consecutively with no rest or pause in-between.

All 8 rounds should take no more than about 40-60 seconds. It is not done slowly with concentration on balance but much faster to assist water movement down through the gastro-intestinal system.

Benefits

Tadasana strengthens the muscles of the intestines and rectum. It stretches the intestines, has positive effect on the spinal column and removes any obstruction in the nerve endings.

Tiryaka Tadasana (Side Bending Stretch Pose)

Method

1. Stand with your feet shoulder width apart. Interlock your fingers.

2. Inhale as you raise your arms up over your head, palms facing upwards.

3. Exhale as you bend to the right side.

4. Inhale as you straighten-up to the centre, then exhale as you bend over to the left side.

5. Inhale as you straighten-up to the centre position.

6. Keep your breathing normal when you practise this asana. Ensure that you don't hold your breath at the time of bending on either side.

Repeat bending to right and left 7 more times without any pause in between. All 8 rounds should take no more than 60 seconds.

Kati Chakrasana (Waist Rotating Pose)

Method

1. Stand with feet shoulder width apart. Inhale as you raise your arms to the level of the shoulders.

2. Keeping the feet flat on the floor, exhale as you twist the upper body to the right side, wrapping the right arm behind the waist and the left hand onto the right shoulder. Turn the head fully to the right to look behind.

3. Inhale back to the centre position.

4. Exhale as you twist your upper body to the left side, wrapping the left arm behind the waist and the right hand onto the left shoulder.

Benefits

This asana is beneficial for the spinal column, waist, back, pelvis and joints.

Tiryaka Bhujangasana (Twisting Cobra)

Method

1. Lie on the floor on your stomach, forehead on the mat, hands placed by the chest, feet apart. Have the toes curled under and the heels raised up.

2. As you inhale, push up raising the head and shoulders, straightening the arms. Ensure that the pelvis is touching the ground.

3. As you exhale, twist the upper body to the right, turning the head as well to the right, to look over the shoulder at the left foot.

4. Inhale as you come back to the centre position.

5. Exhale as you twist the body around the left, looking over the left shoulder at the right foot.

6. Repeat the right and left twists 7 more times without a break, on the last exhalation, coming down to the starting position.

All 8 rounds should take no more than 60 seconds.

Udarakarshanasana (The Abdominal Massage Pose)

Method

1. Squat on both feet, place the hands on knees. Inhale at this centre position.

2. Exhale as you twist the upper body and head around to the right, dropping the left knee onto the floor while pushing the right knee over towards the inner left thigh, exerting pressure on to the lower abdomen.

3. Hold this position for a few moments. Then, while inhaling, come back to the centre position.

4. Exhale as you twist to the left side, dropping the right knee on the floor. While twisting, push the left knee towards the inner right thigh, exerting pressure on to the lower abdomen.

5. Hold the position for a few moments and then while inhaling, come back to the centre position.
   Do 7 more twists to each side without any rest. All 8 rounds should take no more than 60 seconds.

There are several sphincters/openings present in the food pipe, between stomach and anus. Performing these asanas during shankha prakshalana, opens and closes them appropriately, aiding in digestion. Practicing the asanas during shankha prakshalana, loosen the sinews and the saline water passes through to the anus, from where it is then expelled.

After doing these five asanas as described above, drink 2 more glasses of the saline water and repeat all the five asanas 8 times each. Finally, drink 2 more glasses of saline water and repeat the five asanas 8 times each.

In this way, after drinking a total of 6 glasses of saline water (and performing the asanas after every 2 glasses) go to the toilet. If the bowel is evacuated easily, it is good. If not, don't worry - drink one more glass of the saline water and go to the toilet. Ensure not to strain when clearing the bowels. This technique will clear the bowels completely and also increase the volume of urine passed.

Precautions

1. The procedure should be done in the morning on an empty stomach.

2. You must rest in corpse pose for at least one hour after doing this kriya.

3. Do not drink water for the next three hours. It is advisable to eat either khichree, a porridge made of rice or yellow lentils with a spoonfull of clarified butter or ghee in it, the meal should be taken after around one hour of completing the procedure (after having rested in the corpse pose

4. If necessary, doing this kriya once a week is sufficient and should be practiced under the supervision of a trained yoga teacher only.

Poorna Shankha Prakshalana

Poorna shankha prakshalana is a potent practice which cleanses the body thoroughly - it is quite a long and psychologically challenging event. It is therefore advised that it should be performed no more than twice a year, except under exceptional circumstances, and according to qualified guidance. Normally, the appropriate time to do this is when the season is about to change. At the end of winter, it is good to strip off the cold season's accumulation of intestinal mucus and to give the body a 'spring cleaning'. Similarly, end of summer is also a good time to prepare for the coming winter. What differentiates laghoo shankha prakshalana from poorna shankha prakshalana is that in poorna shankha prakshalana, one keeps drinking and exercising, drinking and exercising the same set of 5 asanas until you pass out water as clear as when you drank it. However, this must be done under the guidance of a trained yoga practitioner.

Poorna shankha prakshalana is a very strong and effective practice. It's like exhaustive cleaning of the motor car - scrubbing and cleaning every nook and cranny with a toothbrush and then blowing out the small valves and openings, putting it back together, resting for a while till things settle, and then initially, driving carefully to 'run in'. But if you do that too often, the engine just becomes 'over serviced' and worn out.

Great care, therefore, must be taken in choosing a day for the event, which must not be too cold or hot and neither the day which has changeable weather since the newly cleansed system is vulnerable to chill and infection for the first 24 - 48 hours.

Precautions

1. In case of any injury or ulcer in the stomach or intestines, this kriya should be done only after proper consultation with a doctor and a trained yoga teacher.

2. Patients of hypertension may use plain tepid water instead of saline water.

Physical Benefits

1. A large number of diseases are caused by the accumulation of toxins in the intestines. The purpose of this kriya is to cleanse the bowels and hence purify the blood. This in turn helps get rid of all diseases that are

caused by impurities in the blood, bringing about an extraordinary improvement in the body.

2. Varisara Dhauti is an excellent cure for chronic dysentery, indigestion, esophageal reflux, irritable bowel syndrome and other problems of digestion. This kriya streamlines the functioning of the entire digestive system and prevents renal infections and calculi.

3. If a healthy person practices this kriya, the mind and body are filled with immense positive energy. So, it is beneficial not only for the unhealthy person but is also useful for healthy people.

Spiritual Benefits

Along with cleansing of the body, this kriya has great spiritual benefits too:

1. It is mandatory before undertaking advanced meditation techniques like kundalini yoga.

2. If you are serious about yoga sadhana, then this kriya is a must for you, as it has a deep impact on the mind and prepares both body and mind for meditation.

3. There is a deep connection between the mind and body - an ill mind makes the body weak and increases its vulnerability to disease. On the other hand, many diseases of the body stem from problems of the digestive system. If the digestive system is faulty, the mind too gets distressed. Shankha prakshalana is a powerful yogic tool for strengthening the digestive system.

✳ VAMAN DHAUTI (KUNJAL KRIYA)

It is not possible for a sick mind or a sick body to meditate. When there are impurities in the body, it is not possible to awaken its latent energies. A healthy mind dwells in a healthy body, therefore yoga first deals with the cleansing of the body - the cleansed body then leads to a healthy mind. Body is the gross form of mind whereas mind is the subtle form of body – both are deeply interrelated.

Several techniques have been described in yoga for cleansing the body of all impurities, giving rise to good health. Vaman Dhauti is one such method described in shatkarma. Its primary objective is to cleanse the food pipe and stomach, thereby removing impurities from the upper part of the body.

Method

1. Sit in crouched position (the posture of sitting on one's feet), near a sink or a suitable place outside in the garden or near an open drain.

2. Drink 6 glasses of saline water (proportion of 1 teaspoon salt in 1/2 ltr. water) as quickly as you can. It is important to drink these in a quick succession.

3. Lean forward, place the index and middle finger of your right hand into your mouth, rub the back of the tongue. Ensure that the nails are short and clean.

4. This will cause vomiting (which is called the 'gag reflex' in medical terminology) and all the water from the stomach will be thrown out in a quick series of gushes. Maintain the pressure on the tongue till all the water in the stomach is thrown out.

Benefits

1. This kriya controls and cures stomach acidity and dyspepsia.

2. It also cures problems caused due to infections in the food pipe and helps in curing cough and breathing related problems.

3. The sinews of the stomach walls are exercised in this procedure, thus making them strong and healthy.

4. Vaman dhauti (kunjal kriya) cleanses the stomach. If gastric functioning is not optimal, the food does not get broken down completely. This consequently affects the digestion happening in the small bowel. The ultimate scenario is – the food rots in the intestines. This gets compounded, as one keeps on eating more and more food. The rotting food is more likely to lead to breeding of worms, which cause further rotting of the food. The entire process will inevitably lead to gastro-intestinal diseases like acidity, dyspepsia (burping and nausea), flatulence, dizziness, headache, etc.

5. Stress and tension leads to formation of mental knots, blockages - vaman dhauti not only cleanses the stomach but also relieves one of stress and tension. After doing vaman dhauti just twice or thrice, a person who is depressed, sad or irritable feels much lighter. Is it not a wonderful technique? You cleanse the stomach - and end up benefitting the mind as well!

Spiritual Benefits

These techniques have been developed by the rishis after extensive research. If our aim is to meditate, then all the bodily systems should be working perfectly. Vaman dhauti is for cleansing the stomach and removing all toxins from it. If a person with excessive acid formation does vaman dhauti, the fluid thrown out from the stomach has a greenish hue.

Precautions

1. Wash the hands and make sure the nails are carefully trimmed.

2. Do not eat anything for 20 minutes after doing the kriya.

3. The first time you should do the kriya under the guidance of a yoga teacher.

4. If you suffer from asthma, stomach ulcers, heart disease or hernia, then do not do the kriya without consulting a teacher.

5. People suffering from acute acidity should refrain from doing this kriya.

Precautionary Note

This kriya can be practiced once a week, and in special cases twice or thrice but only after consultation with a trained yoga practitioner. People suffering from flatulence, indigestion, acidity or other stomach related problems should do this kriya every day on an empty stomach. If done after shankha prakshalana, this kriya becomes even more beneficial.

❊ KAPALABHATI (PURIFICATION AND VITALISATION OF THE FRONTAL LOBES)

In Sanskrit, kapala means 'forehead' and bhati means 'shining'. So kapalabhati is also known as 'shining forehead'.

Method

1. The technique can be practiced in either standing or sitting position. Sit on the floor in sukhasana (cross legs) or padmasana (lotus posture).

2. Place the hands on the knees. Keep your back straight all the time. The exhalations should be forceful but the inhalations should be automatic and effortless.

3. Contract the abdominal muscles forcefully, at the time of each exhalation. Repeat this in quick succession, performing fifteen or twenty sets at a stretch.

Remember, rhythm is more important than speed. Do twenty cycles in the beginning - then take a pause for slow deep breathing. Repeat another set of forceful exhalations. Develop this practice slowly so that you can do it for 30 minutes to one hour.

Benefits

There are quite a few benefits of this pranayama:

1. Kapalabhati is a cleansing breathing technique, which cleanses the respiratory system and the lungs.

2. It also purifies the blood in the body as well as increases the oxygen level in the body through the cells.

3. Kapalabhati is good for digestion.

4. This kind of forceful exhalation and contraction of the abdomen strengthens the muscles of the abdomen.

Spiritual Benefits

1. The effective breathing technique prepares the mind for meditation.

2. It is good for energising the mind and for energetic mental work.

Precautions

1. Kapalabhati pranayama should be done with caution - if you feel dizzy then stop the practice immediately and lie down to take rest.

2. Patients who have high blood pressure should do it very slowly and for a limited time.

3. Someone who has undergone surgery should wait for six months before beginning this practice.

Trataka means gazing steadily at one point without blinking. It enhances focus and increases supply of blood to the eyes - cleanses & strengthens them. The most popular and pleasant trataka technique is to gaze at the naked flame of a candle.

During the practice of trataka, one must try not to blink the eyes for as long as possible – the eyes may become watery but with practice one can keep the eyes fixed at one point without blinking for a longer period of time.

Trataka is of two types: internal and external. External trataka can be done on a candle flame, statue, flower, deity, clouds, or the sky, whereas in internal trataka, one focuses on either the blankness within or create a mental picture of the guru or deity and do internal trataka.

Physical and Spiritual Benefits

There are immense benefits of doing trataka as physically it strengthens the eye muscles, at the mental level it deepens concentration, and helps in the awakening of ajña chakra.

CHAPTER 11

Secrets of Yoga Nidra
R e v e a l e d

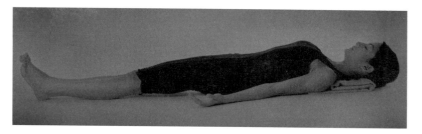

The most potent mantra for living life is that if you live free of worries, you will live longer; if you live a stressful life, you will die early. So, if you wish to die early then go ahead and worry a great deal! Keep awake at night! On the contrary, if you wish to have a long life, rid yourself of all types of worries.

To be completely free of stress, it is necessary that you act on my advice and make it a part of your lifestyle, attend satsang, spiritual discourses, keep the company of sages and live the wisdom received from them. It is also very important to understand the significance of simran because it can free you of worries and tensions. So, learn this technique from the master.

In his well known poem - 'Gobind ke gun gao sadho', Guru Arjan Dev has extolled the virtues of simran. In fact, this life has been granted to you for simran only, but how is a stressed mind going to remember God? For this, there is a new technique called yoga nidra. Usually yoga is done when awake, but there is a type of yoga which can be done only in the sleeping state. One is either awake or in deep sleep, but in yoga nidra one is fully awake and yet the body and mind experience all the symptoms of deep sleep.

Yoga nidra rests and relaxes the body. You may feel that you rest at night when you sleep, but if after sleeping all night you wake up feeling tired and dull, then your sleep is meaningless! The reason is that you keep dreaming in your sleep, tossing and turning in the bed - you may feel warm or thirsty, the mosquitoes might be troubling you, or maybe you are so tired that your body is aching too much to allow sleep! Even if you fall asleep, you sleep fitfully and keep dreaming, and then the alarm rings, you have to get up, and the daily chores start. If after sleeping for seven hours you wake up tired and irritable, then it is a sign of stress in the body.

Many people suffer from spondylitis, sinus, breathing problems, headaches and persistent colds. Women always have a headache! Even this is a sign of stress. More often the atmosphere at home is not harmonious - this is because you do not know how to manage your relationships - you have great expectations, or you are always criticising the other person. And when the mind is in tension, how can the body be healthy?

People often suffer from indigestion and acid reflux - this too is caused by mental tension. It is the tension of the mind that descends into the body and takes the form of disease. In fact, causes of around 80% of the diseases can be traced to the mind; diseases do not travel from the body to the mind! Therefore, if we keep the mind healthy, the body will also be healthy.

Yoga nidra gives you composite health and complete relaxation. At the level of the body, it relaxes the muscles and nerves; at the same time it also accords mental and emotional rest.

Now the interesting part is that yoga nidra is to be practiced while lying down. But don't think that you are going to get a chance to sleep, as you don't have to fall asleep, rather, you have to be fully alert. It is a highly effective practice through which you can relinquish physical and mental stress. Only a tension-free mind can do simran. If the shoulders are tense or the neck is stiff, a person will not be able to sit straight, as required for meditation. If the knees are stiff or hurting, you cannot sit cross-legged. And if the posture is not still, how will you meditate?

Concentration and Meditation

The first requisite therefore, for meditation is that your body should be absolutely still. Some people keep moving like a rocking chair! Why? Because their mind is oscillating all the time, and the reason for this is the unhealthy body. That is why I say that yoga nidra is an invaluable tool for students who lack concentration and who are unable to remember their lessons in spite of studying properly.

Life has become synonymous with tension in modern times. But meditation cannot be done in a state of tension. So, I suggest you first do yoga nidra for 40 minutes; it is an easy procedure and you have to do it lying down - so you will not have any problems of sitting for too long either. Yoga nidra is a panacea for people who suffer from insomnia or fluctuating blood pressure. When the mind is free of all tensions and the body too is healthy - you sleep well; deep sleep is very important to keep the body healthy. It is in deep sleep that the endocrine system secretes the chemicals and hormones that are essential for our wellbeing.

If you are unable to sleep well, the endocrine system is unable to function properly - this leads to diseases. Therefore, it is important for the body to get the necessary rest in order to stay in good working condition.

If you take medicine for indigestion, it will settle the problem for the time being, but if you do not settle your mind, the condition will recur and you will need repeated medication. Why do you suffer from recurring headaches? Because of stress! Why is the heart rate increased and the blood pressure imbalanced? Because of stress! People follow religious practices, they pray and recite the Hanuman Chalisa, but I wonder in what frame of mind they do all this. They are either lacking in faith or devotion, or they do not fully trust god – why else would anxiety persist? If you have strong faith, why would you be anxious? But we do the two things together - we perform religious rituals, and we worry!

A man once asked me to bless him with all the happiness and comforts of life. I replied that if just my blessings could give all the comforts, I would bless the whole world sitting in my ashram in Gannaur! But by asking for blessings, you cannot receive any such gifts of happiness. In reality, you have to generate happiness. And for this, the essential requirements are - wisdom, discretion, reflection, contemplation, knowledge, and a peaceful mind. Live life in a regular, controlled and disciplined way – it will prove to be extremely beneficial for you.

These days, even walking on the road has become dangerous. All the vehicles stop at the red light but as soon as the red light turns amber, the people start honking – their faces are so tense, so harried, so full of stress! Ready to fight and argue and even kill! It seems you do not wish to live. If you did, you would not be ever-ready to fight and shout and get angry. It seems the agenda is to worry yourself to an early grave! How to teach such a person the true art of living!

Modern man faces several psychological problems - neurosis, phobia, mania and fear - because of which he cannot lead a normal healthy life. Some people fear the darkness, while others have a fear of insects; some even fear the colour red! Some suffer from claustrophobia while others are scared of heights.

These fears and phobias are a great hindrance to meditation. Yoga nidra brings the practitioner out of these phobias, fears and manias. It not only relaxes the body and mind, but makes them disease-free. The greatest advantage of yoga nidra is that it is a comprehensive, unique meditation technique in itself, based on tantra.

Those who understand the religious rituals know that in any oblation, first the place is prepared for the ceremony. Reciting mantras, the fingers are placed on 12 different parts of the body: head, forehead, ears, nose, eyes, face, shoulders, chest, knees, feet, hands etc., while reciting the appropriate mantra for the purification of that body part - this is referred to as 'vinyaasa' – and without this, the oblation does not begin. So, first of all, the body of the person who is going to perform the yagna is purified.

Yoga nidra is also based on 'vinyaasa' - and after the physical and mental relaxation, the practitioners experience tremendous inner depth. This feeling of depth is achieved by making contact with the various levels and layers of the mind.

Three Levels of Consciousness

Consciousness exists at three levels: waking state, dreaming state and the state of deep sleep. In the waking state - the conscious mind is at work; in the dreaming state - the subconscious mind is at work, and in the state of deep sleep - the unconscious mind is at work. But most important thing to note here is that within these three states – waking, dreaming, sleeping – you just keep jumping from one state to another.

In fact, most people are either awake or sleeping. But between the two there is a state when one is neither fully awake nor fully asleep - this state is extremely subtle – now the question is how to grasp this subtle state? Yoga nidra takes you into this very subtle state.

Process of Yoga Nidra

❋ STAGE 1: RELAXING THE BODY

Lie down with the feet slightly apart and leave them relaxed. Close the eyes and face the open palms upwards. You may use a thin pillow if required. Lie straight and relax. This is a wonderful technique – no sitting up straight, no vajrasana, no siddhayoniasana – it is done lying down! The whole body is to be relaxed.

❋ STAGE 2: MAKING THE RESOLUTION

When the whole body is fully relaxed and mind too is fully relaxed, then you plant the seed of resolve in the subconscious mind.

The resolve must be the expression of transformation that you desire in your life – wisdom, samadhi, good health - whatever you wish to achieve, especially in the realm of spirituality. The resolve should be pertinent to your spiritual evolution as the worldly pursuits have already caused stress in the first place. So, yoga nidra must always include an auspicious resolution.

After the first stage of relaxation, when you are asked to make your resolve, do so in short and precise sentences, as follows:
"May I attain great spiritual heights."
"May I receive my Guru's blessings."

"May I attain samadhi."

"May I be healthy and energetic."

Be focused, do not prolong the resolve into a lengthy discourse and don't let the mind oscillate.

In the first stage of yoga nidra, the entire consciousness is focused on the body - you are totally relaxed and you should keep reminding yourself that you will not fall asleep and will follow the instructions carefully. It is very important to invoke this affirmation otherwise as soon as you start yoga nidra, 'Yoga' will disappear and all that you will be left with is 'Nidra' – sleep!

However, even if you fall asleep during yoga nidra, it is alright – may be you have not slept for long - due to stress. If someone falls asleep during yoga nidra, it means that he needs to sleep. In yoga nidra you will get what you need, when you need it. At the same time, it is important to start the practice with the determination that 'I will honestly follow the instructions and not fall asleep.'

The best way to know that the conscious mind is not working is that the physical sensations will cease to exist. You do not even realise where you are; you cannot tell whether the breeze is fragrant or has an awful smell. As sleep approaches, external sensations and impulses diminish – all that remains is the ability to hear.

You might have, at times, noticed that even if you call out to a person in deep sleep, he wakes up. This is because even in the sleeping state, sound travels far with you. Therefore, you should not do yoga nidra on your own – rather use the recorded format of yoga nidra.

✳ STAGE 3: MOVING CONSCIOUSNESS TO DIFFERENT PARTS

In the third stage, you are asked to take the consciousness to different parts of the body and finally to the breath.

The movement of the inhaled breath is felt in the abdomen, chest and throat. You may feel it in the abdomen and chest, but it is difficult to sense it in the throat. Yoga nidra has various levels of practice; as your ability grows, you progress to higher and advanced levels.

It is important to keep the body absolutely still and the eyes closed during yoga nidra - there should be no movement at all.

The next stage is that of visualisation. When you dream, are you aware that you are dreaming? No! You do not even realise that you are dreaming; as soon as you realise, the dream breaks. One cannot dream in the waking state – this happens only when you enter the unconscious state of sleep.

During the visualisation process, when any object is named, you have to recall all the memories associated with that word. The mind has memories of past experiences - of feeling heavy as well as light, of extreme heat and extreme cold. When we make contact with the deepest layers of the mind, these memories are to be invoked in order to make contact with the hidden samskaras, to bring them to the surface.

After experiencing these physical sensations, you are again taken back to the level of body awareness. Finally, yoga nidra comes to an end and you are asked to sit up.

Important Guidelines

All the steps in yoga nidra are scientifically designed and you should not bypass any step. It is an easy method but you must follow it carefully and with understanding. Take care to ensure the following:

First, the body should be absolutely still and the eyes should be closed right through the entire process. Second, if you do not feel any sensation in a particular part of the body when asked to concentrate on it, do not get tense. Third, make a resolve right at the beginning of the practice by saying, "I am going to start yoga nidra and that I will not fall asleep", and repeat this resolve thrice.

The resolve is made twice - once at the beginning and then when you reach the last stage of yoga nidra. And each time the resolve is made, it is to be repeated thrice because it takes some time for any thought to take root in the subconscious mind. The subconscious mind exists at a very deep level, so in order to reach it, it is necessary to repeat the resolve thrice.

When you reach the last stage of yoga nidra, you will once again be asked to repeat the resolve thrice. Be careful in choosing an appropriate resolve, as whatever you wish for will certainly come true.

Power of the Subconscious Mind

The subconscious mind is extremely powerful and has infinite potential. If one uses this power correctly, one can achieve anything one desires in this very lifetime. If you aspire to become a sage, attain self-realisation, or desire for samadhi – it will become reality.

When you first make the resolve, it is akin to sowing a seed. Later, when you repeat the resolve, it is like watering the seed. If today you make a resolve to get enlightened, do not expect to become one tomorrow! It does not take a few weeks or months but a few years for an acorn to grow into a mighty oak.

Nevertheless, the miraculous potential of yoga nidra is very unique – it is possible that the transformation that would have taken a few lifetimes, takes place in a few years only. Now, this is not a bad bargain at all that something which would have required several incarnations can now be attained in just a few years! This is indeed the best gift you can give yourself – you can use the power of the subconscious mind for your evolution and welfare.

So, yoga nidra gives you rest and relaxation, relieves physical and mental ailments and helps you sleep well. It also increases your ability to learn. If you want to learn a new language or anything new, it enhances the ability to grasp and remember.

Experiments of this Ancient Technique

In 1975, an experiment was conducted in the control room of a test lab in Belgrade, in which ten children were guided into the state of yoga nidra. Then French, Spanish and Math books were read out to them. The next day, when the children were fully awake, they were asked questions from the matter read out to them the previous day. 40% of the children were able to answer correctly; this figure increased to 60% the next week and to 80% in a month.

I would like to make it clear that this is not hypnotherapy. In yoga nidra, you remain fully alert and aware, and you move from one stage to another with awareness. You remain alert while listening to and following the instructions.

Yoga nidra is not auto-suggestion. Try it out for yourself - you will see that as soon as the body relaxes, you will fall asleep. At times you will reach the breathing stage and then fall asleep while doing the counting. This is why it is recommended that you never do yoga nidra on your own even if you know and remember all the instructions; the instructor's voice is a necessary input.

I envisage a day when there will be beds instead of desks in schools. Children will do yoga nidra, and in that state they will be taught a subject for just two hours. All the learning and knowledge will be directly transmitted to the subconscious mind. And then in two hours, school will be over! Sing, dance and go home! This age is for enjoying life – not for stress, strain and tension.

Teaching the subconscious mind is as easy as teaching the conscious mind is difficult. A practical angle of yoga nidra is that it increases the capacity to absorb knowledge from external sources. Practice yoga nidra for a few months regularly and not just for a few weeks. Only then you can realise the changes brought about by it.

Yoga nidra takes you into a state in which you receive wisdom from supreme divine sources. It is an instrument for gaining rest, relaxation, deep sleep and good health. It is a unique method of meditation which helps you access even worldly knowledge very easily. There are a hundred possibilities - it is up to you how and where you apply them.

Life is a boon and a blessing. Live, but with awareness! God has given you the gift of life - do not disregard or disrespect it. Keep the mind and body healthy - keep your mind empty so that God's name can reverberate in it. You need to create vacuum in your mind to let the divine name resonate. And when the vacuum is complete - you will chant the name once but it will echo ten times.

Yoga Nidra & Freedom from Stress

Dharma is life. It is your basic nature. Eating, sleeping, all actions, behaviour, in fact what kind of dreams you see – their analysis and understanding too is dharma. It is extremely difficult to directly enter a meditative state until and unless the body and all levels of the mind and emotions are uncluttered, unburdened and free. There is a method, a sequence, a discipline and determination that is required to attain this state.

The human body is actually a composite of five koshas: first is annamaya kosha, the gross body made up of five elements; second is pranamaya kosha, science calls it the bioplasmic body; third is manomaya kosha; fourth is vigyanamaya kosha and fifth is anandamaya kosha. Most people are born in ignorance, live in ignorance and die in ignorance - unaware, unwise and unintelligent – this is how they live and die. Observing the lives of people, often it seems that they have a human body, but at a deeper level they are animalistic. An average human life exemplifies this perfectly. In childhood one eats, drinks, sleeps, plays and goes to school. Then between the age of 10 and 14, the hormones get active - girls start menstruating and boys develop facial hair, testosterone in boys and progesterone and oestrogen in girls – these are the hormones which bring about the changes.

When menstruation starts, it is not only the body of the girl, but also the mind that begins to change. Before the age of 10, the awareness of gender is definitely there, but there is no attraction for the opposite sex. Why? Because the chemicals that cause these changes are not present till the age of 10, therefore the body and mind chemistry is not fully developed. When this happens, there is a change in the physical and mental body; one becomes aware of one's gender and a simple and natural attraction develops for the opposite sex.

The institution of marriage was set up by society, so that when the time comes, this basic attraction and instinctive need for sex finds a legitimate expression and does not become uncontrolled, as that could lead to an immoral life and ills in society.

After the age of 32, the natural process of degeneration starts in the body - pranic energy decreases, making the body lethargic. And the undisciplined and uncontrolled lifestyle that you have adopted will only hasten the aging process and shorten the lifespan. By sleeping late at night and rising late in the morning, you go against the rules of nature, adding further afflictions to the body. All the endocrine glands produce and secrete their chemicals - growth hormones, GH, ACTH, Thyroxine, etc., - during the sleeping state. If you are awake at night (in the pursuit of work, business, money or sex), you are forcing your body to act against the laws of nature. Know that by doing so, it is none other than your body that suffers pain and disease.

Appropriate and balanced lifestyle is crucial for overall wellbeing – this includes regulated intake of food, apt and pertinent day to day behaviour and interactions with people.

If you live a balanced life, you can even live for 500 years. But if you do not value your body and health, nature is certain to punish you. There was a time when childhood, youth and old age were well defined. Today it is not so - children have become old and the youth lack energy and vitality. Hypertension, heart disease and digestive problems have begun to arise in childhood, which were once considered diseases of old age. Asthma is now increasingly prevalent amongst kids. By violating the rules of nature we are punishing no one but ourselves.

It is sad that a life that should have been lived with joy and bliss has become a burden and suffering. You complain about the smallest little problem and get tense over it. Even school-going children are subject to the stress of competition and lofty expectations. "Son, you must top in studies. If you do, we will buy you a scooter, a video game... whatever you want." Either you bribe the child or threaten him! Little wonder then that very young child of yours, who cannot handle the stress of not fulfilling his/her parents' expectations, commits suicide.

Stop and think about what you are doing. What sort of parents are you? Why do you not realise that every child has his own individual capacity and intellect? His academic performance depends on his intellectual level; his performance in sports and creative arts depends on his mental makeup. But parents insist on a certain percentage of marks - the child goes to school burdened by this stress imposed by none other than his own parents!

Look at your hand: are all five fingers equal? Will you apply the rules of socialism to make all the fingers equal? Will you cut them to size? Will you chop off all your fingers and become handicapped in the quest for equality? No, you don't do any such thing; you accept the fact that the five fingers are different. Similarly, every child has some special qualities and talents - but it is not necessary that they may be to your liking.

Symptoms of Stress

To live a life full of bliss and joy, you will have to completely unburden your mind and intellect. You are living under such a huge burden of stress that this very burden also starts to affect your health. Tension and stress have become your best pals and you cannot deny that. Many people say they do not have any tension. I will tell you a few symptoms of stress and you check out if any of these is present in you. If they are, then you are tense, otherwise you are tension-free.

- You suffer from frequent headaches.
- You need digestive pills to digest your food.
- You don't get deep sleep.
- Your blood pressure is above 120/80.
- You have diabetes.
- Your pulse and heart rate are abnormal.

If you have any of these symptoms, then you are living a stressful life. Tension has a direct effect on the body - under its influence, the hypothalamus – the master computer of the body – sends such commands to the body that various diseases start to take root. Some people live in a state of constant tension and anxiety – tense if they do something and tense if they don't; tense in sending the children to school and tense in their coming home; tense if something needs to be bought for the house and tense on learning that it now costs more…the list is endless!

If the children respect and care for you, it is good. But if they don't, then you should be ready to live an independent life once the son gets married; let the children live their own independent lives. You don't stop interfering in their lives and then you are unhappy. You want to stay in the ashram so that your mind becomes peaceful. No! You better stay at home and correct your bad habits! Live your life in a disciplined, wise and discrete manner and your home itself will become your heaven. As long as you harbour dislikes, you will find peace nowhere. To lift the burden of emotions and stress from the mind, yoga nidra is the unique path of dharana, dhyana, samadhi.

Yoga Nidra & Freedom from Fear

Regular practice of yoga nidra relaxes the muscles, mind and intellect. And besides this, you would also experience absolute tranquility. When you reach such a state of total relaxation, you can release all afflictions lying deep in the subconscious and unconscious mind. It is in this state of complete relaxation, the stage of visualisation which is the most important step in yoga nidra becomes possible. In this step, you see every scene on your mental screen and experience the emotions associated with it. Whether it is a rising sun, a rose or a lake, when you visualise a scene at the level of consciousness, the experiences and samskaras associated with it are also aroused.

Once I was conducting yoga nidra session in England. After the session, a lady walked up to me and said that when I (Gurumaa) said 'beach', she was able to visualise a beach, but along with it she was also reminded of an unpleasant experience. She said, "Once I was holidaying in Spain with my family - we had all gone to the beach. It was very crowded which made me feel a terrible sensation of fear and suffocation, as though I was trapped. So, with the mention of 'beach' in yoga nidra, this experience became alive, but as soon as the next instruction to visualise the rising sun came, I felt as if the rays of sun are healing my body and making me healthy." So, in this way, with the help of yoga nidra, you can eliminate neurosis and phobias. There are various types of fears that people experience in life like, someone is afraid of darkness, someone suffers from claustrophobia and so on – everyone is grievously affected with the subtle fear of death. All such types of fears can be uprooted with the regular practice of yoga nidra.

Yoga Nidra & Creativity

When you experience physical, mental, emotional and intellectual rest and relaxation in yoga nidra, complete equilibrium is established between the mind and the brain. The brain has two parts - a right and a left half. All aspects of our life are controlled by the brain. Creativity – music, painting, art, singing, dance – all these talents take birth in the brain. If your brain is not in harmony, all these faculties will lie dormant in you. If you wish to be an accomplished singer, musician, dancer, writer, author, teacher, student, meditator, or rajyogi, you can develop the required skills very easily through the medium of yoga nidra. This is because yoga nidra energises and stimulates the dormant areas of the brain which play a role in developing these talents.

You will be astonished to know that today even western science accepts that we use only up to 6% of our total brain capacity; the remaining 94% remains unused. A scientist as great as Albert Einstein, who made huge contributions to the world of science, used only 7% of his brain! You can now very well imagine how little of the brain capacity a normal person uses.

When you stimulate the dormant cells of brain through yoga nidra, it brings forth astonishing results - remarkable enhancement of memory, assimilation, resolve, determination and talents besides the unleashing of suppressed and latent capabilities. These days many people are afflicted with insomnia – it has becomes the curse for the modern age. People go to bed but toss and turn, unable to sleep. From drinking warm milk to taking a shower – all remedies are tried, but to no avail. Insomnia is a curse that destroys health, and deep sleep is a blessing which we have lost due to tension, greed and ambition. Yoga nidra is an elixir for this deficit.

A lady has enquired that she falls asleep during yoga nidra, which should not happen, so how should she correct it. Even if you fall asleep during yoga nidra, it is a good thing, because you are entering that aspect of nature's cycle where whatever is needed is supplied. If stress and tensions have ruined your health and sleep, then yoga nidra will first fulfil that deficiency. You can also relieve all psychosomatic diseases with the help of yoga nidra. Many people suffer from depression, lack of confidence, low self-esteem and various fears or phobias. In yoga nidra, when you are in a state of total relaxation and you resolve to be healthy and fearless, the resolution seeps into the subconscious and brings forth the results.

Conscious Mind versus Subconscious Mind

The sub-conscious mind has a profound effect on the conscious mind. While doing yoga nidra, you plant the seed into the sub-conscious mind like, 'I want to be fearless', 'I want to be healthy', 'I want to be a seeker',

'I want to attain samadhi'. The resolve made at that time settles in the sub-conscious and then directly affects the conscious likes and dislikes, choices, decisions and behaviour. In my opinion, yoga nidra is essential for men, women, children, and the elderly….everyone. The wonderful thing about yoga nidra is that you can treat and cure yourself.

In 1992, an experiment was conducted in Australia, on patients suffering from acute pain due to fractures. In clinical trials, they were made to do yoga nidra - as a result, their need for pain killers was slowly reduced until it was not required anymore. The bones had not healed fully, but the pain was greatly alleviated.

It is interesting to note that physicians, who have understood the technique of yoga nidra, are actually prescribing and recommending it to their patients. At one time, there was a proposal to start yoga nidra in Russian schools. But then Russia broke up and the proposal did not find favour with the new regime. However, as long as it was practiced, encouraging results were seen in the childrens' intellectual and learning capabilities.

Yoga Nidra – An Unusual Science

Today, the technique of this unusual science of yoga nidra is being used to train astronauts in India. This technique can be used to awaken and arouse the sixth sense, extra-sensory perceptions and even telepathic abilities. In case of any system failure in the craft, any technical fault or loss of contact with the ground control centre, the space travellers are trained to communicate mentally in order to solve the problem – not with instruments, but with mind to mind contact.

Extra-sensory perception and clairvoyance are not imaginary abilities – they are totally realistic. Many of you have experienced that sometimes i.e. when you harbour a query in your mind, right then you get an answer from me. A few letters arrived today asking how it happened that the question that was in their mind was answered.

Whatever you think reaches me – this is no great power. Even you can achieve it. When a person whose mind is totally relaxed, listens to a religious discourse or a spiritual talk, it verily bears fruit. Such a person does not listen like a parrot, nor does he listen for entertainment – for him it becomes a medium of transformation. Only 5% of what I say reaches you, the rest just evaporates! You are unable to actualise the wisdom you gain because the mind is scattered. This scattered mind can be consolidated with yoga nidra.

Your prayer will become a potent tool when you pray with a peaceful and relaxed mind - it will bestow exhilarating joy and unusual experiences. If you are a devotee, your devotion will deepen; if you are a spiritual aspirant, your contemplation will improve; if you aspire to do yogic sadhana, your sadhana will intensify.

Earlier I have explained about the pranic body. If the pranic body is healthy and progressive, you acquire miraculous powers - in this world, miracles are revered, not the wisdom. So, I am telling you what you want to know. There is no need to run after miracle-mongers - practice yoga nidra to experience the evolution of miraculous powers within yourself. But beware - when a rajoguni or tamasic person acquires these powers, he ends up destroying himself. So before acquiring the powers, the mind should be satvik and rooted in godliness. Actually, those lacking these qualities are also bereft of the powers, where as in the case of satvik person who is rooted in godliness, and who is totally surrendered to God, the same powers get awakened easily.

Once Guru Ramdas was offering service at Harmandir Sahib where a pond was being dug and the foundation of the temple was being laid. Devotees of Guru Nanak had come from far off places to offer their services. There was a lady from Afghanistan, who would ever so often raise her hand in the air and shake it. The sangh found it very strange, so someone asked her what she was doing. "Nothing. My child is sleeping, so I am rocking his cradle."

"Your child is sleeping in the cradle? Where?"

"In Afghanistan."

"Where in Afghanistan?"

"In Kabul?"

"How is that possible? You are rocking your child in Kabul from Amritsar? You are a liar."

But the woman insisted she had no reason to lie. So Guru Ramdas was approached and asked if this was possible.

"Of course it is!" said Guru Ramdas. "The power of the mind is limitless. The mind doesn't know the boundaries and limitations of body, place, country or time – these hold no meaning for it. If the pranic energy is developed, nothing is impossible."

I urge you to awaken these mysterious powers lying dormant within you. Through the medium of these powers, you can rise above an animalistic life and live like a celestial being. When you can be a rishi – then why live like an animal, why live like an ordinary person oscillating in laughter, anger, tears, sex, greed etc. There is nothing that you cannot achieve! But for now you are concerned only with money. Well, even wealth can be earned!

Role of Focused Mind in Earning Material Wealth

When you manage your business or profession with a disciplined and focused mind, you get innovative ideas leading to success. Any successful businessman or industrialist is successful because he has one-pointed and determined mind - he works with determination and patience. A person lacking these two qualities can never be successful in any field. Earn wealth or power – whatever you desire. But at the end of the day, you must realise that wealth can buy you objects, not peace of mind. Power can suppress others, but of what use is it if it cannot control your rebellious mind? Power is worth having if it leads to real and actual progress. Be emancipated!

Live life with wisdom. I reiterate! Wealth is not bad, power is not bad, and material pleasures are also not bad - but you must understand their limitations; they cannot give you more than what they stand for. Tread the path of truth. Understanding and worshipping the truth, as you progress in life, you will be filled with fearlessness and eternal joy – which will always stay with you and will never abandon you.

Physical Pain in Yoga Nidra

You may experience severe pain during yoga nidra - this is not due to any uncomfortable position of the body. The pain was already present in the body but was ignored and therefore had not been felt earlier. Yoga nidra helps you to become aware of all suppressed pains. When you practice at home, ensure that you use the recording and know this that the success mantra of this technique lies on single factor - simply following the instructions.

Those who have been practicing yoga nidra for some time, feel an electric current in the body when they do yoga nidra – as though a current has swept them from head to toe. Such an experience is not problematic and it is quite natural for this to happen. That is why usually it takes few minutes to come out of yoga nidra – like the way it takes time to move into yoga nidra slowly. That is why you are asked to come out of it slowly. Regular practitioners of yoga nidra enjoy the experience so much, that they do not want to come out of it - they like to stay in it longer.

There are about 10 to 12 different types of yoga nidra practices in which the instructions change. We move gradually from the body to the heart and then to the internal organs, and then we become aware of the heartbeat.

A doctor is able to diagnose the disease only by checking the pulse. In the same way, a stage comes in yoga nidra when you hear the heart beat – at first it seems strange and novel. Anything novel is astonishing - the mind is amazed by what is happening and it starts contemplating. That is why I told you in the beginning to not to go into analysis. Just comply with the directions if you can, if you cannot, don't worry. You do not need to worry about anything. If you cannot feel the part you are asked to, do not let your mind play games. Otherwise, instead of relaxing, you will become more tense. Let whatever is happening - happen.

Yoga Nidra and Insomnia

Sleeplessness or insomnia is considered a disease in psychology, as many physical and mental diseases are associated with it. It causes irritability, sadness and tension. We wonder why someone is irritable and tense, but it can be put down to lack of sleep or constipation. This is how we end up disregarding insomnia, which is in fact, a matter of grave importance.

However, if sleeplessness is the reason then the best way to solve it is yoga nidra. Listen to the yoga nidra CD – in the first stage, I have explained what yoga nidra is, and then comes the complete technique of yoga nidra. All you have to do is lie down keeping the body relaxed, as in shavasana. Then just follow the instructions, and you will find that by the time yoga nidra is over, you will already be asleep.

Once your sleep pattern is set right, the same yoga nidra can be used to increase your power of concentration and to experience deep meditation. If you do it just before going to bed at night, you will sleep well. If you do it during the day, your memory and concentration levels will go up. In other words, if you do yoga nidra during the day, it increases your daytime concentration. If you do it before sleeping at night, then it cures insomnia and fitful sleep. You will get deep sleep and dreams will not delude you. Often people do not enter a state of deep sleep and keep wandering in the dream state. They run around in the daytime after material objects, and at night they run around in their dreams after the shadows of the mind. Lack of deep sleep will never allow you to be in good health and live a normal life.

I recommend yoga nidra to everyone, regardless of whether you are an insomniac or not. If you want to improve your concentration or memory or creativity – yoga nidra is a must for you. Every profession needs creativity today. The more creative you are, the better your professional prospects will be. What is the difference between a tailor and a fashion designer? They both stitch clothes, but the designer charges lakhs for a piece while the tailor only a few rupees for the same piece. What sets them apart? The fashion designer is professionally better off, because he has creativity on his side. Most designers only design the clothes – they are, after all, stitched by the tailor who knows how to stitch but lacks the designing skill.

Yoga nidra enhances your creativity, therefore it has multiple applications. Practice yoga nidra every night before going to bed – the whole technique takes just 45 minutes. Great sleep, great health and a great life! Live life joyfully! It is God's gift!

Audio & Video Collection of
Discourse/Meditation/Sufi/Devotional
By Anandmurti Gurumaa

Discourses A.C.Ds, V.C.Ds, DVDs

1. Astitava Se Mulakaat (5 DVD SET, includes MP3)
2. Guru GIta (25 DVD SET)
3. Guru Ke Gyana Ka Adhikari Kaun (2 ACD SET)
4. Jaap Sahib (25 VCD SET / 13 DVD SET)
5. Jeevan Ka Vigyana (4 DVD SET / 8 VCD SET)
6. Kabir (10 DVD SET, includes MP3)
7. Kaisi Aarti Hoye (2 VCD SET)
8. Ki Jaana Main Kaun - Baba Bulleh Shah
   (15 VCD SET)
9. Krishna Premanjali (5 DVD SET, includes MP3)
10. Kya Hai Sadhta (VCD)
11. Manotantra Vigyana (VCD)
12. Mann Ka Saatvik Aahar (VCD)
13. Raj Yoga (13 ACD SET)
14. Rasiya Sang Rang Barse
    (5 DVD SET, includes MP3)
15. Shankracharya (28 VCD SET)
16. Shivoham (30 VCD SET)
17. Shrimad Bhagavad Gita
    (71 DVD SET / 136 VCD SET / 16 MP3)
18. Tanaav Ko Kahein Alvida (5 DVD / 10 VCD SET)
19. Tu To Mann Ke Mool Mein (VCD)

Discourses A.C.Ds & V.C.Ds - English

1. God: Mystery or Reality
2. Know Your Mind
3. Shakti - An Ode to Women

Meditation A.C.Ds & V.C.Ds

1. Beyond Boundaries (Hindi & Eng)
2. Mudra (Hindi & Eng)
3. Pranav (Hindi & Eng)
4. Ram Ras
5. Sacred Spaces
6. Shiv Naam Omkar
7. Simran (Punjabi)
8. Sparsh (VCD)
9. Stuti Sutra
10. Tratak
11. Urja (Hindi & Eng)
12. Waheguru (Punjabi)
13. Yog Nidra for Youth (Hindi)
14. Yoga Nidra - Part 1 (Hindi & Eng)
15. Yoga Nidra - Part 2 (Hindi)
16. Zikr

Devotional A.C.Ds & V.C.Ds

1. Ananda Stotras
2. Aanando
3. Anhad
4. Baawari Jogan
5. Chamkan Taare
6. Chants of Krishna
7. Des Begana Hai
8. Dilbar Ki Karda (2 VCD SET)
9. Fragrance of Love
10. Gayatri Mantra
11. Ishq Hi Maula
12. Kahe Kabira (2 ACD SET)
13. Kripa
14. Maha Mrityunjaya
15. Mool Mantra
16. Nanak Aaya
17. Odyssey of Love
18. Rangi Re
19. Saajanra (VCD)
20. Saanwal Saanwal
21. Sajda
22. Samarpan
23. Sheikh Farid
24. Shiva's Ecstasy
25. Shivoham (2 ACD SET)
26. Shoonya
27. Shri Rama Stuti
28. Waheguru Jaap

New Age Music for Cause

Suno Suno Meri Aawaaz

Poetry A.C.D

Rumi - Love at its Zenith

MP-3

1. Jaap Sahib
2. Japji Sahib
3. Rehras Sahib
4. Shalok Mahalla Novan
5. Shankaracharya
6. Shivoham
7. Ki Jaana Main Kaun

For more information & comprehensive collection, please logon to
www.gurumaa.com., or place your order on call: 09896263821 / 0130 - 2216500 / 0130 - 2216501

Books of Wisdom by Anandmurti Gurumaa

These books are transcriptions of the extempore talks given by revered Anandmurti Gurumaa from time to time at various places. Books are one of the many ways of chronicling the wisdom that flows from the master, acting as a catalyst for the true seeker.

1. Aatam Bodh (Hindi, Marathi, Telegu)
2. Anhad Ki Dhun (Hindi)
3. Antar Drishti (Hindi)
4. Antar Ke Pat Khol (Hindi, Guj.)
5. Ath Kahe Narad (Hindi)
6. Bhaj Govindam (Hindi)
7. Chinmay Ki Aur (Hindi)
8. Dhamm-Jeevan Aadhar (Hindi)
9. Going Beyond The Mind (Eng)
10. Govind Naam Mere Pran (Hindi)
11. Gyan Kshitij (Hindi)
12. Health And Healing Through Yoga (Eng)
13. In Quest Of Sadguru (Eng)
14. Kabira Ram Yun Sumariye (Hindi)
15. Karun Hridaya (Hindi)
16. Know Thyself (Eng)
17. Naame Ke Swami (Hindi)
18. Prem Diwani Meera (Hindi)
19. Prem Ka Chhalakata Jaam (Hindi)
20. Prema Bhakti - Ek Utsav (Hindi)
21. Quotes Of The Unquotable (Eng)
22. Rehras Sahib (Punjabi)
23. Rumi Aur Main (Hindi)
24. Rumi's Love Affair (Eng)
25. Sadguru Kaun (Hindi)
26. Sadguru Pura Paayo (Hindi, Punjabi, Guj.)
27. Shakti (Hindi, Eng, Guj., Telegu)
28. Shivoham (Hindi)
29. Sutras For Transcending Indulgence (Eng)
30. Swar-Madhushala (Hindi)
31. The Compassionate Buddha (Eng)
32. Truth Exposed (Eng)
33. Yog Se Aarogya (Hindi version of Health & Healing Through Yoga)
34. Yuktaahar (Hindi, Telegu)

E-books

You can buy & download the e-copy of this book and other english books by Anandmurti Gurumaa at www.gurumaa.com.

Rishi Chaitanya Ashram
Energy-field for your conscious evolution

Just as flowers need the right climate, the right care to bloom and blossom, so do we need the conducive environment and guidance to evolve our consciousness and tread the path of emancipation. Presence and guidance of the master is extremely necessary on this path, as it is the master who dispels the darkness of ages and awakens the eternal light within the seeker, by sharing his own fiery light of wisdom. For this journey from unconsciousness to consciousness, from periphery to the centre, from illusion to reality, abode of the mystic master Anandmurti Gurumaa, offers the perfect climate.

A hub of an immense positive energy, Rishi Chaitanya Ashram is a panacea for the modern world, blinded by storms of lust, greed, attachment, ego - all get respite and relief once they arrive in the Ashram and work towards their evolution. It is a cosmic field of energy - energy that acts as a catalyst for self-realisation. It is an energy-field where under the guidance of Gurumaa, seekers explore the inner world, understand the mechanism of mind and consciously strive to realise their true nature.

Retreats are the time to treat yourself with meditation, yoga, solitude, wisdom and a lot more in the evolutionary ambiance of the Ashram with the mystic master Anandmurti Gurumaa. There are many opportunities to participate in the retreats which are organised around the year. Their details are published in the monthly magazine of the Ashram, Rishi Amrit and online at www.gurumaa.com.

❧ Stay at Ashram
Stay at the Ashram is a unique experience. It offers a simple, uncomplicated and spiritually rich environment. Rooms may be reserved by phone, via e-mail, or online at www.gurumaa.com. A minimum 15-days advance booking is required. Call 0130-2216500, 2216501, 09896263821 or e-mail your room booking request at info@gurumaa.com. For more details, visit www.gurumaa.com

❧ Address
Rishi Chaitanya Ashram
NH-1 Gannaur, Distt. Sonepat, (Haryana) - 131101

HINDI MONTHLY
MAGAZINE
FROM
RISHI CHAITANYA ASHRAM

RISHI AMRIT

Inspiring Revolution in Human Consciousness
Insight
Dhyana Sutras
Exclusive Articles based on Gurumaa's Discourses
Scientific Revelations for Spiritual Evolution
Events & Programmes in Ashram
Details of Meditation Retreats
and much more...
to help you soar higher in inner sky...

To subscribe logon to www.gurumaa.com,
or call 09896263821 / 0130 2216500-501

Logon to Gurumaa.com

your quest ends here...your journey begins now!

Watch Online Discourses

Shop at ease from online store of Cds/Books

Get Free Subscription to G-Sandesh to receive messages from the Master

Subscribe to monthly magazine from Rishi Chaitanya Ashram

Stay updated with upcoming events & programs

Be a part of Shakti mission - Empowering & Educating girls

Contribute online

www.gurumaa.com